RUGBY
AND
ALL THAT

Martin Johnson

with

David Norrie

coronet

CORONET BOOKS
Hodder & Stoughton

First published in Great Britain in 2000
by Hodder and Stoughton
First published in paperback in 2001
by Hodder and Stoughton
A division of Hodder Headline

10 9 8 7 6 5 4

A CIP catalogue record for this book
is available from the British Library.

ISBN 0 340 79254 X

Typeset in Rotis Serif by Palimpsest Book Production Limited,
Polmont, Stirlingshire
Printed and bound in Great Britain by
Clays Ltd, St Ives plc

Hodder and Stoughton
A division of Hodder Headline
338 Euston Road
London NW1 3BH

RUGBY
AND
ALL THAT

To my mum

CONTENTS

ACKNOWLEDGEMENTS

GRATEFUL THANKS to David Norrie, my friend, journalistic colleague and former London Scottish full back, without whose diligent research I would now be approximately halfway through chapter two. His assistance on the behaviour of amateur rugby players at the bar was particularly helpful, not so much because I myself had no experience in this area, but because of his remarkable (and sometimes dangerous) morning-after memory. Thanks are also due to John Ireland for his evocative caricatures.

PHOTOGRAPHIC ACKNOWLEDGEMENTS

The author and publisher would like to thank the following for permission to reproduce photographs:

AllSport, Colorsport, Mary Evans Picture Library, Hulton Getty Collection, Mark Leech Sports Photography, Popperfoto.

All text illustrations are by John Ireland.

CHAPTER 1

LIFE WITH LEICESTER'S TAMIL TIGERS

THE NIGHTMARES ARE LESS INTENSE NOW, but they never really go away. I still wake up, sobbing incoherently in the middle of the night, while my wife mops my brow with a cold flannel and whispers soothing words of comfort. 'There, there, now. It's all right. Cusworth and Wheeler aren't here now . . . it was just a nasty old dream.' But I still insist that she checks under the bed, or inside the wardrobe, just to make absolutely sure.

I remember my time as the *Leicester Mercury* rugby correspondent (1979–86) as though it were yesterday, starting with the occasion – on my first away trip – when I foolishly informed certain members of the pack that I was not entirely sure of the difference between a ruck and a maul. 'Why don't we show you?' they said, and for the next fifteen minutes I assumed the curled up hedgehog position while the lads unselfishly went out of their way to further a young reporter's education.

Hotel guests leapt for cover as the lads charged through the lobby either squeezing me like an Amazonian anaconda, or spitting me out like a farmer's threshing machine. I somehow survived eight years of this, an era when a local newspaper's rugby reporter was not so much in the running for a journalistic award as a Victoria Cross. However, being a not unwilling participant in what at that time constituted letting your hair down after a match, I dedicate this book to my liver.

'Mr Wheeler! Mr Wheeler! I appeal to you. As a responsible member of the team. Would you please come down at once!' The voice belonged to a Heathrow hotel deputy night manager, and I groaned in fearful anticipation of what was about to happen to him as he strode into the resident's lounge at around three o'clock in the morning in a final attempt to put a stop to that gentle rugby players' pub game known as 'bar diving'.

The Leicester Tigers were on their way to the Middle East for a two-match Easter tour, and were preparing in the traditional fashion of their era. Bar diving, many of you will doubtless remember, involved clambering onto the counter top, hurling yourself into outer space, and into the linked arms of waiting colleagues. If fortified with sufficient quantities of strong ale, it was not uncommon to expand the routine with some spectacular back flip, hoping for a few extra marks for artistic impression. The only flaw in this game, was an occasional reluctance of the reception committee to keep their arms linked at the crucial moment, although the diver was usually sufficiently anaesthetised to pick himself up for another go even after rupturing a spleen and splintering several ribs.

Mr Wheeler, captain of Leicester, captain of England, and respectable businessman, was perched unsteadily on the bar counter, with one foot in an ashtray, and the other lodged against the beer pump, a 100 metre runner hoping to explode out of the blocks. As befitting a future Justice of the Peace, he weighed up the night manager's impassioned plea with all the gravity he could muster. From the look in his eyes, however, the more experienced among us could tell that he was about to reach for the black cap.

2

'Mr Wheeeeeeluurrggggh!' was the last thing the hapless night manager uttered as the Leicester and England hooker, without even letting go of his pint, launched himself straight on top of him. There has not been a bigger rush of escaping wind since Captain Oates opened the flap of Scott's Antarctic tent, and when Wheeler finally peeled himself off, the night manager had been turned into the shape of an old LP cover. It was a lesson to us all. Never appeal to a rugby player's sense of reason at three o'clock in the morning.

Despite having booked into a hotel, no one was allowed to go to bed, or indeed to stop drinking on the morning flight to Bahrain. I didn't even stop despite going to sleep for a couple of hours, a period which one of the prop forwards managed to utilise for the tour party's continuing amusement by topping me up – by clamping a couple of fingers across my nose and inserting a funnel into my mouth – with red wine. My somewhat unsteady entry into Bahrain was further complicated by the absence of the required journalist's visa and, although the lads tried to spring to my defence – 'If you saw the crap he writes, you'd never describe him as a journalist' – I found myself not only under arrest, but in imminent danger of being bundled on the first plane back home again. If only . . .

I didn't realise quite how popular I was until the boys greeted my release with such delight that they insisted on holding a party in my room. With twenty-six tourists in the squad, there was scarcely enough space for everyone, so they thoughtfully made some by removing the bed to the balcony, putting the TV set in the bath (full, of course), and consuming the entire contents of my mini-bar. 'Just put it down as "entertaining" on your expenses,' they said. 'I don't find this entertaining at all,' I said.

That evening, the lads got wind that one of our number – let's call him Hall – had notched up the first score of the trip with one of the local ladies, and decided to pay him a visit. How he came to be duped by an appalling imitation of a

3

middle-eastern accent croaking 'Room service' through the bedroom door, God only knows, but he made the fatal mistake of opening it, and the other twenty-five members of the tour party poured into the room and invited the terrified female occupant to 'just carry on as though no one's here'.

Having previously informed the captain and tour manager of my own less than complimentary opinion of the behaviour of rugby players on tour, I bumped into Mr and Mrs Hall in the hotel coffee shop the following morning. 'Jonno,' he said, 'you're bloody right. This lot want locking up. They're a bloody disgrace.' Twelve hours later, in a context too bizarre to explain, I was within half a centimetre of being totalled by a flying bottle (full) of HP sauce. I looked around to identify the perpetrator, but I knew almost before I looked. It was Hall.

The following night, we attended a poolside reception which involved an official visit and speech from a fully fledged sheikh. A teetotaller, he was reduced to near incontinence by liberal spiking of his orange juice, and was still giggling as he was hurled into the swimming pool. It was only my own insistence that the frantic arm-thrashing and incoherent gurgling noises coming from beneath the dish-dash, was more in keeping with someone drowning than having a whale of a time, that saved his life.

It would be wrong to suggest that there were no moments of calm and tranquillity during Tigers' away trips, as I remarked to one of the centres as we dangled by our ankles over the Avon Bridge in Stratford. I asked Tim Buttimore, who is now the agent for England lock forward Martin Johnson (no relation), what he had done to warrant his upside down position, but he could think of nothing other than committing the heinous crime of being a back when two inebriated prop forwards happened to be looking for a bit of sport.

Quite how no one ever died on one of these trips is still beyond me, as I mentioned to one of the players during a stumble through the streets of Swansea one Saturday night while a Mini hurtled past doing around 85 mph. It was not so much the occupants themselves I feared for, or indeed innocent pedestrians, as the Leicester committee man stretched out on the roof, using one hand to cling on, and the other to wave to anyone he recognised.

I never made the return coach journey from an away trip on the roof, but articles of clothing often did, and the centre skylight was a favourite for wedging my trousers. One day, they did not survive the G force, and were last seen flying backwards down the M69. Likewise, the club president of all people, once saw fit to end a game of pass the reporter's shoe by lobbing it out of the same orifice, and I'm not sure I ever returned home with the same amount of gear I set off in. When the wife opens the door to find someone clad in jacket, underpants and a single shoe, you have a hard time convincing her that the trip was actually quite enjoyable. I still have that old jacket, one of the pockets – despite the best effort of Sketchley the cleaner, who did a roaring trade with me every Monday morning – still impregnated with a combination of ground pepper and the contents of a soda siphon.

I did manage to claw back a little of the cash expended at the dry cleaners by not having to pay for my evening meal on a Saturday night, largely thanks to Hall's propensity for falling asleep face down in his curry. The rest of us would thank the manager profusely for an unsurpassed vindaloo, point to the comatose Hall, and say, just before departing, 'It's okay, he's paying.'

The Tigers, in common with most rugby clubs of that non-professional era, had any number of methods of not paying for their evening meal, including the sad occasion when their away trip return stop at a country hotel coincided with a wedding reception. That part of the bride's cake not hauled into the bar as a tastier accompaniment to the ale than a packet of pork scratchings was left dripping from the velvet curtains. Heaven forbid the poor girl was marrying a rugby player.

Then there was that first away trip when I was introduced to left-handed drinking. Anyone caught picking up their pint with their right hand incurred a heavy penalty, none more savage than when the chairman of the fines committee had purchased several bags of vinegared whelks, and ordered them to be tipped into my pint for drinking down in one go while standing on a table. I may have tasted fouler potions in my lifetime, but none that spring to mind.

There was never a moment when you could afford to drop your guard, as I was reminded during a stopover at a steakhouse, and found that my portion of sirloin had not been cooked as specified. After sending it back for the third time, I was invited into the kitchen to do it myself, and returned in triumph to thunderous applause. I was just about to tuck in when my attention was (purposely) distracted, and I turned back to an empty plate. One of the props (why was it always a prop?) was standing on the table with an exultant glint in his eye, and swallowed my steak with a single satisfied gulp. That was the same trip on which the club, for the first and only time, hired a coach with an on-board toilet. It was immediately rendered U/S by the front row using it as a receptacle for my notebook. There were, of course, predictable comments as to it being entirely appropriate for someone who wrote much, er, crap.

And yet, in a way, the memories are almost always fond ones. We once had a Friday night fixture at Ballymena, which involved getting the game out of the way as soon as possible, and then repairing to the clubhouse for the real purpose of the mission. Anyone who looked remotely connected to Leicester was issued with a dozen cloakroom tickets, each one of which constituted a free pint. Then, when you tried to exchange one, an Irish voice would invariably say, 'No, no, save those for later. Have these ones on us.'

They drove us back to the hotel at about three in the morning, where they'd plonked £100 behind the bar, just to get us re-started, and they picked us up again for a lunchtime session at the pub the following day. After that, they drove us to the airport for more drinks at the bar, and when we tried to board the chartered Dakota, we could hardly get on it for the number of cans of beer they'd stowed away to see us nicely back across the Irish Sea.

Lord knows what the newspapers would make of it all today, especially as the Tigers team invariably comprised well-known public figures. Dean Richards was anything but the dour figure he cuts now as the Leicester coach, as the Scots discovered after a Murrayfield international. He and John Jeffrey, the Scottish flanker, took the Calcutta Cup out on the town with them and returned it in such a flattened state of disrepair that it was renamed the Calcutta Tray.

Clive Woodward, the current England coach, will doubtless thank me for not revealing one or two stories he was involved in, although Clive's erratic behaviour was mostly confined to on the field rather than off it. Accident-prone is not the word. Brilliant player though he was, he managed to lose crucial games for Leicester, England and the Lions in a pretty short space of time. When the Lions were beating South Africa in Port Elizabeth with a few minutes to go, Woodward casually sidefooted a ball into touch and, while he was still wandering back infield, the Springboks not only took a quick throw-in, but scored the match-winning try. During a John Player Cup semi-final against Coventry, Woodward had apparently put Leicester into the final with a late interception, only to look around in triumph a few yards from the line, fall over, and lose ball. His *pièce de résistance*, however, came in Cardiff in 1981, when England were about to end an Arms Park drought stretching back to 1963. Deep into injury time, with England a point ahead, the Welsh scrum half Brynmor Williams essayed a then legal dummy pass from the base of the scrum, and Woodward galloped up so far offside that he very nearly collided with the Welsh full back. As Steve Fenwick lined up the winning kick, Billy Beaumont, legend has it, put a compassionate arm around the disconsolate Woodward behind the posts, looked him in the eye, and said, 'Clive, you've done so many wonderful things for England that I don't want this to get blown out of proportion. As far as I'm concerned, and I can say this on behalf of all the boys, I think you're a complete prat.'

How many memories? Jerry Day, the club secretary, and a legend at Welford Road for the way he could clear an entire clubhouse with a single fart, once decided – at the age of about sixty – that the modern player could not bar dive with the same panache as in his day, and tried to clear about seventeen chairs – Evil Knievel style – in the upstairs bar. They needed a crane to clear up the mess, and never did find his glasses.

That downstairs Nissen hut could tell a few tales as well, not least the day Dusty Hare was thrown out by the sponsor because he had been selected for the 1983 Lions and was exercising his first-time Lion prerogative not to play for Leicester for the remainder of the season. Les Cusworth led the rest of the players out in protest, and upstairs to mingle with the punters in the public bar.

It was always the case in those days that a supporter could watch the game, repair to the bar, and find himself being served by a Hare, a Woodward or a Wheeler. Nowadays, the players have their own special lounge, well away from the public gaze, and are more likely to be drinking Gatorade or glasses of milk than pints of ale. You are no longer liable to see the captain of England peeing up against the goalposts at half past eleven as his wife patiently revs up in the car park, and these days, local newspaper reporters presumably return home with their trousers on, but you can't tell me that the modern game is anything like as enjoyable as the old one.

CHAPTER 2

OH, WHAT A TANGLED WEBB

RUGBY FOOTBALL: a game for hooligans played by gentlemen, for whom – until the ghastly advent of professionalism, beep tests, pasta diets and early nights – it was an exercise in identifying who could sing the dirtiest song after consuming a minimum twenty pints of ale, followed by a jolly amusing attempt to frighten the occupants of a family saloon with several hairy bottoms pressed up against the back window of the team coach on the way home. And the man we have to thank for this is, as every schoolboy knows, William Webb Ellis.

Or is it? Uncharitable though it may seem to deny William his place in history, there is actually more compelling evidence that the Scandinavians pipped the Scots in inventing golf, or that a very large amphibious camel-like creature is swimming around in Loch Ness, than there is for Webb Ellis to be recognised as the founder of rugby. Nonetheless, the plaque in the Doctor's Wall at Rugby School, a building that attracts countless annual visitors, reads:

> *This stone commemorates the exploit of*
> **WILLIAM WEBB ELLIS**
> *who with a fine disregard for the rules of football as*
> *played in his time first took the ball in his arms*
> *and ran with it thus originating the distinctive*
> *feature of the rugby game*
> *A.D. 1823*

An impressive epitaph by any standards, but the only historical evidence to support this assertion is contained in a letter written to the Rugby School magazine, *Meteor*, by an unnamed eye-witness, later shown to be a former pupil, one Matthew Holbeche Bloxham. Neither could it be claimed that it was exactly fresh in Bloxham's memory, having been penned a mere fifty-seven years after the event. There is little doubt that Rugby School gave the game its name, and its laws, but the case for a folk hero as well is rather less compelling.

Mr Bloxham's epistle was written on 16 October, 1880, and the writer was merely one of countless contributors to the argument then raging – largely in the columns of the *The Standard* – over the game's true origin. He gave a description of a game played at Bigside in 1817, followed by an account of the incident forever linked with William Webb Ellis. However, Bloxham omitted to say exactly how he had come to witness Webb Ellis's charge over what has now come to be known as the gain line, which would have been of no small interest given that he had actually left the school three years earlier. Perhaps it was Old Boys' Day.

The Old Rugbeian sub-committee were undoubtedly good men and true, but judging by the way they swallowed Bloxham's claims without the raising of a single inquisitive eyebrow, there was little evidence of an ancestral bloodline to Jeremy Paxman or John Humphrys. It seemed pretty clear to them that someone sometime at Rugby School must have picked up the ball and run with it, so why not William Webb Ellis?

It is worth reiterating that the game being played at Rugby at the time was not soccer (it was played with an oval ball for a start) and it was not until 1863 that rugby and soccer became distinguishable. The game played at Rugby at that time made it perfectly allowable for players to catch a ball which had been punted in the air – in fact, that was the very idea. It was a bit like the equivalent of the modern 'mark', with no opposition player allowed to molest the marker until he had either punted it or placed it for someone else to kick. Anyone catching the ball and then running forward with it was a potential suicide case, as he would have been promptly buried under something a touch more serious than one of today's modern rucks. The game at that time could quite often comprise 300 players.

Bloxham's letter of 1880, nine years after the formation of the Rugby Football Union, reads as follows:

In the latter half of 1823, some 57 years ago, originated, though without pre-meditation, that change in one of the rules which more than any other has since distinguished the Rugby School game from the Association rules.

A boy by the name of Ellis – William Webb Ellis – a town boy and a foundationer, who at the age of nine entered the school after the mid-summer holidays in 1816, who in the second half-year of 1823, was, I believe, a praeposter [prefect] whilst playing for Bigside at football in that half-year, caught the ball in his arms. This being so, according to the then rules, he ought to have retired back as far as he pleased, without parting with the ball, for the combatants on the opposing side could only advance to the spot where he caught the ball and for someone else to kick. For it was by means of these place kicks that most of the goals were in those days kicked, but the moment it touched the ground the opposite side might rush on. Ellis, for the first time,

11

disregarded this rule, and on catching the ball, instead of retiring backwards, rushed forward with the ball in his hands towards the opposite goal, with what result as to the game I know not. Neither do I know how this infringement of a well-known rule was followed up, or when it became, as it is now, the standing rule.

Bloxham also gave an account of football played at Rugby.

Few and simple were the rules of the game: touch on the sides of the ground was marked out and no-one was allowed to run with the ball in his grasp towards the opposite goal. It was football and not handball, plenty of hacking but little struggling. [A bit like watching Scotland, then.] As to costume, there were neither flannels nor caps, the players simply doffed their hats and coats or jackets, which were heaped together on either side near the goals until the game was over.

The year 1895 was a crucial date in rugby's attempt to settle the argument about who had actually invented it. A subcommittee of the Old Rugbeian Society was set up in another attempt to consider the historical evidence, by which time Bloxham had been dead for seven years, and Webb Ellis for twenty-three years. There is also a certain amount of evidence that the sub-committee members themselves (H.F. Wilson, H.H. Child, A.G. Guillemard and H.L. Stephens) had all but passed away in the brain-cell department when it came to the conclusions they arrived at from the evidence presented to them.

Firstly, there were already two books in existence under the authorship of Mr (later Sir) Montague Shearman entitled *Athletics and Football* and *Football: Its History For Five Centuries* (1885), neither of which contained a single reference to a William Webb Ellis. The same applied to a volume on football's origins written in 1892 by the Rev. F.M. Marshall, but the Old Rugbeian sub-committee dismissed their conclusions, or their omission of Webb Ellis at any rate, as misleading.

They heard from a Mr T. Harris, who recalled that 'picking up and running with the ball was distinctly forbidden. I remember William Webb Ellis perfectly. He was an admirable cricketer, but generally regarded as inclined to take unfair advantages at football.'

The committee reminded Harris that he was several years Webb Ellis's junior, and had neither reasons nor opportunities for closely observing his manner of play. Harris replied: 'The cry of "Hack him over" was always raised against any player who was seen running with the ball in his hands.' A

footnote in the report on Harris's testimony reads: 'This proves nothing. It was a common cry for years when running with the ball was allowed by the laws.' Ergo, the committee appears to have been suggesting that Harris's memory might have been playing him up.

By far the biggest doubt about the Webb Ellis legend, however, was raised by Thomas Hughes, author of *Tom Brown's Schooldays*, who became a pupil at Rugby nine years after Webb Ellis left. Hughes told the committee: 'I don't doubt Matthew Bloxham was right that "running in" was not known in his day, but the "Webb Ellis" tradition had not survived to my day.' In other words, less than a decade after Webb Ellis had supposedly left an entire school aghast with his revolutionary tactics, it was never mentioned during all Thomas Hughes' years at Rugby School.

'In my first year, 1834,' Hughes, who was captain of Bigside, told the committee, 'running with the ball to get a try by touching down within a goal was not absolutely forbidden, but a jury of Rugby boys of that day would almost certainly have found a verdict of "justifiable homicide" if a boy had been killed running in. The practice grew, and was tolerated more and more, and indeed became rather popular in 1838/39 from the prowess of Jem Mackie, the great "runner-in" . . . Jem was very fleet of foot as well as brawny of shoulder, so that when he got hold of the ball it was very hard to stop his rush. He was a School House and Sixth Form boy, therefore on the numerically and absurdly weak side in those most exciting matches of that time. He was M.P. for Kircudbrightshire in later years and a very useful but silent member.'

The sub-committee's conclusions were published in the form of a booklet produced on the school's own printing press two years later – and two years would have to be a minimum timespan you would need in order to work out how to answer any awkward inquiry along the lines of: so, have I got this right? An eighty year old bloke writes a letter to a school magazine detailing an event which took place three years after he left, but which no one else at the school has any recollection of ten years later, and you believe it?

There were more balanced investigations in the Middle Ages, when anyone drowning during a dunking was acquitted of being a witch, and anyone failing to drown was declared guilty as charged and burned at the stake. Nevertheless, the sub-committee's conclusions were as follows:

1) *In 1820, the form of football in vogue at Rugby was something approximating more closely to Association than what is known as Rugby Football today.*

2) *That at some date between 1820–1830 the innovation was introduced of running with the ball.*

3) *That this was in all probability done in the latter half of 1823 by Mr W. Webb Ellis, who is credited by Mr Bloxham with the invention, and whose 'unfair practices' were the subject of general remark at the time.*

Football as played by hoi polloi at that time was often little more than a mass mêlée with a pig's bladder in which rival gangs of urchins knocked lumps out of each other as a kind of ritual precursor to a monumental piss-up down at the local ale house, but it was more refined in the public schools, and gradually evolved into two separate games – one involving the hands, and the other, the feet.

Rugby School also did the game the service of providing, in 1845, a proper set of rules and a scoring system, with caps awarded – as they were to be for internationals – to those players of exceptional talent. They were the only ones allowed to run around following the ball. The duffers were consigned to defending, which meant hanging idly around between the goalposts, like smokers gathered behind the bike-shed, until danger threatened the line.

distinct forms of football in the English
the dribbling and kicking game where use of
was strictly forbidden (Eton, Harrow, Charterhouse)
handling game in which there was also kicking and
ooling (Cheltenham, Marlborough, Rugby). The game at
Eton developed into association football, and the game at
Rugby became rugby football.

The new trend did not find favour with everybody. However, despite bemoaning the fact that 'our game has been abused because it permits running with the ball', one correspondent to *The Field* magazine drew a similar conclusion to Corporal Jones's of the Warmington-on-Sea Home Guard – 'It is said our game is barbarous because it permits brute force to form so important an ingredient. Is it not because of brute force that no nation in the world can face us at the bayonet?'

Between 1750 and 1840, at Charterhouse, Eton, Harrow, Westminster, Winchester, Shrewsbury and Rugby, football was adopted and run by the boys themselves, often in defiance of the masters, and was yet another way in which older boys asserted their dominance over the younger ones. The fags were forced to play, but their participation was restricted, mostly to keeping goal. At Winchester, the fags were made even more conscious of their inferiority by being forced to stand in lines, as the most convenient way of marking the pitch.

Another factor which might have contributed towards the curious conclusion of that Old Rugbeians' investigation into the game's origins was the growth of football in the north, and its success there – among people they considered to be the great unwashed – was perceived as a threat by the southern toffs. Their game, in effect, was beginning to spin away from their own control, hijacked by ruffians and urchins, and against all their own values of snobbery and social hierarchy. Therefore, by promoting the Webb Ellis theory, it is not unreasonable to speculate that their overriding motive was to consolidate and re-assert their proprietary rights to the game in the face of a powerful threat by the (to them) distasteful ranks of coal miners and manual labourers. Had it not been for the Webb Ellis business, in fact, rugby football – horrible though it is to contemplate in alickadoo-land – might even have become a working-class sport.

In the RFU Centenary History, HQ declared: 'Whoever "invented" Rugby Football, this entirely amateur game in a sporting world that has become too generally an insult to the word sport as a result of its tawdry professionalism, has given the greatest delight to generations healthy in mind and body. The game has become part of the national life of the countries all over the world where it is played, and is an unrivalled character builder, where giving is so much more important than taking.' A quarter of a century later, rugby union joined the professional ranks and went on the 'take'.

By 1923 the version of events as promoted by the Old Rugbeians had become so imbued in the game's doctrine that a special centenary match was arranged for the Close played between combinations of England/Wales v Scotland/ Ireland on 1 November. There would have been obvious advantages in holding the game at Twickenham, but this would have compromised the plans of the organisers to treat it more like a private party than a general celebration of rugby. Judging by the clandestine way the whole thing was prepared, the organisers might well have co-opted an advisory sub-committee involving members of the Ku Klux Klan. Rumour had it that the 'celebrations' were in the hands of a joint committee of the Old Rugbeans and a sub-committee of the Rugby Union, but if this was the first recorded gathering of a collection of old farts, they were determined to be silent farts.

Not even an uncomplimentary editorial in the semi-official *Rugby Football* publication had any effect on the let's-keep-this-one-to-ourselves-chaps policy, and applications for information were rarely granted the courtesy of a reply. As for the press, wartime reporting restrictions were applied, and more than one former international found difficulty in obtaining a ticket. One well-known international who did make it to the match was approached by a member of the organising committee while the game was in progress and invited to attend the banquet that evening. He declined, indicating that while the organising committee might be looking forward to consuming their meal by traditional methods, there were other orifices available, one of which he strongly invited them to consider. The match was witnessed by 2000 privileged invitees (including 600 boys) and was won by England/Wales by two goals, two dropped goals and a try (21 points) to two goals and two tries (16). The result would have been the same under today's scoring system, albeit by the narrower margin of 25–24. Despite taking the match back to its perceived historical roots, there was no question of the organisers remaining on site for school dinners, and 200 selected guests took the train back to London for a banquet at the Great Central Hotel in Marylebone.

Being November, something warming was doubtless on the menu, but if indeed the occasion was largely about honouring the memory of Webb Ellis, there might have been some kind of culinary conflict between Lancashire hotpot and Irish stew. There is no surviving birth certificate (in which case Wales might feel inclined to submit a retrospective claim on him) but, although the 1851 census gives his birthplace as Manchester, and the date of birth around mid-November, there is a certain amount of evidence for the fact that Webb Ellis in fact, had Irish qualifications.

Webb Ellis's father, James, was a serving member of the British Army in Dundalk, Clonmel and Dublin during the year of William's birth. There is no evidence to suggest that the family was anywhere other than Ireland that year but, given the political situation involving Ireland and the British government, there would have been every incentive for a young man of William's upbringing to profer somewhere on the British mainland – such as Manchester – as his birthplace instead.

It was not until 1808, when William was a year old, that James left Ireland via a posting to Manchester – the regimental depot – before heading off the following year to the Peninsular War. James purchased a commission in the 3rd Dragoon Guards for the sum of £735 on 14 September, 1809, and when he died on 16 May, 1812, Ann was left with a pension of £10 per year for each of her two sons, William, five, and Thomas, eight. She moved to Rugby where the boys were educated on the grounds of residency.

Rugby School itself is unable to confirm his birth, nor can Oxford University, where, after leaving school in the summer of 1825, Webb Ellis entered Brasenose College. All Rugby School can tell us is that William joined them in 1816 as what was described as a diminutive schoolboy, who was a member of the unpopular Townhouse, which had a reputation for gamesmanship. However, while belonging to the house most associated with underhand tactics inclines you to think he might have picked up the ball and run with it, it would have been more of a stupid thing to do than sneaky – the sporting equivalent of the Charge of the Light Brigade. Bloxham wrote in 1880: 'he did an act which if a fag had ventured to have done, he would probably have received more kicks than commendations.'

Apparently a student of fair-to-average ability, Webb Ellis subsequently took Holy Orders (more evidence – Forgive me, Father, for I have sinned . . .?) and later became the incumbent minister at the church of St Clement Danes in the Strand. There is a plaque there erected to his memory, although not until after the Second World War when it became the church of the Royal Air Force. His actual grave was discovered by the co-author of the *Guinness Book of Records*, Ross McWhirter, at *caveau* no. 957 in Cimetière des Vieux, Château Menton, in the south-west of France. It has since been cleaned up by French enthusiasts and was unveiled in its new pristine state – bedecked with a Union Jack and a Tricolour – in a ceremony including the French Rugby Federation

President, the captain of the French national side and a brass band.

William's father was killed in action at the battle of Albuera, and although there is no record of precisely how, it is known that he received a posthumous award for gallantry – which, in all probability, would have happened to William if he really had picked up that ball and run with it at Rugby School eleven years later.

CHAPTER 3

ENGLAND'S ARISTOPRATS

IF THERE REMAINS A DOUBT about the identity of the founder of rugby football, there is none at all about the most unpopular rugby-playing nation of the last hundred years or more. It is England by a landslide. I remember attending a match in Dublin in the 1990s, and ending up in a pub full of Scottish supporters celebrating their victory over Ireland that afternoon. Standing on a table was a gentleman in a kilt, belting out – to the enthusiastic accompaniment of his chums – a full-throated rendition of the 'Marseillaise' – not 'Flower of Scotland', mark you, but the 'Marseillaise'. And the reason was, as he later told me in a graphic sentence which contained few words other than 'Sassenachs', 'bastards' and an impressive variety of copulatory adjectives, that England had lost in Paris that same afternoon. Scotland beating Ireland was merely a cause for quiet satisfaction, but France beating England was an open invitation for orgiastic celebration. Again in the '90s, an English defeat elsewhere was the catalyst for joyful revelling through the streets of Edinburgh after a Scotland–Wales match, with Celt hugging Celt, and linking hands for a mutual celebration in song. To the tune of 'She'll

Be Coming Round the Mountain', England were raucously invited to find an appropriately vulgar anatomical parking place for their sweet chariot.

Now there are any number of reasons, unconnected to rugby, for England's deep unpopularity among the other home nations – Bannockburn, Offa's Dyke, Agincourt, and the Irish Rebellion among them – but there is also the not insignificant matter of the RFU's natural inclination to regard the rest of the rugby-playing world as some kind of canine deposit on the end of their shoe. From the very moment of their inception, the RFU studied the prefect-fag system of the public schools of their day and concluded that a role as the Flashmans of rugby football would do them very nicely. It worked, as well, and it was not until the pony and trap had almost given way to flying to the moon that the other rugby-playing nations managed to break a structure that kept England in more or less absolute control for almost a century.

They even managed to keep the southern colonial upstarts in their place, long after the likes of New Zealand and South Africa had overtaken the northern hemisphere in terms of playing power; neither was the RFU above cutting off their nose to spite their face. This was manifestly clear from the way they dealt with the increasing strength and success of the northern clubs, mounting the equivalent of a holy crusade against the merest whiff of professionalism, and not much caring about destroying themselves as a playing power for two decades on the moral altar of keeping the game pure.

> *Rugby must always be amateur, which means playing in one's spare time for recreation. If a man wants to play professional rugby, good luck to him. But there is no room for him in our game.*
>
> W.W. (LORD) WAKEFIELD, former England captain and RFU president

In December, 1870, an amalgam of five Scottish clubs – Edinburgh Academicals, West of Scotland, Merchistonians, Glasgow Academicals, and St Andrews – issued a challenge through the columns of *The Scotsman* newspaper to play any team 'selected from the whole of England'. The challenge was taken up by Blackheath, but the Scottish gauntlet was enough to convince many leading figures in the English game that an umbrella association was a good idea, and the secretaries of Blackheath and Richmond duly sent out invitations to other clubs to gather to form a unifying code. Thus, on 26 January, 1871, at the Pall Mall Restaurant in Cockspur Street close to Trafalgar Square, thirty-two representatives from twenty-one clubs assembled for this purpose. It should actually have been twenty-two clubs, but the representative from Wasps managed to turn up at the wrong place on the wrong day. Edwin H. Ash was appointed the first RFU honorary secretary, with the splendidly named Algernon E. Rutter its first president. Rugby School was not represented – it being still eleven years from its elevation to mythical status – although a number of Old Rugbeians were present. In fact, the first five presidents of the RFU were not only all Old Rugbeians, but all London-practising lawyers.

Immediately after its formation, the RFU appointed the first ever of a species that was subsequently to multiply like bacteria in a pond, namely a sub-committee. Charged with drawing up a code of rules, it was an all Old Rugbeian triumvirate of Rutter, E.C. Holmes and Leonard J. Manton. They came up with fifty-nine laws (the first-ever comment is not recorded in the minutes, but it was obviously along the lines of 'Righto, chaps, let's keep it simple . . .') and they were ready for consideration by 22 June. Whether or not they sat down for the first time to the old thespian good-luck message of 'break a leg', Manton duly did – playing football – and as he was the man charged with putting everything down on paper, the original laws of the game were drafted from the horizontal position. Shortly after his death in 1933 at the age of eighty-eight, a letter written by Manton was discovered showing that the other two members of the laws committee had little involvement. 'My colleagues – Rutter and Holmes – finding that I was lying on my back from a football injury, politely told me that, as I was on the sick list, I should prepare the draft rules to give effect to the description of the game then existing at Rugby School. This I did with my own hand, and at a subsequent meeting of Rutter, Holmes and myself, the draft was accepted without any material alterations and was afterwards adopted by the Rugby Union.'

Actually, Manton's colleagues were rather pleased when he became incapacitated and the captain of Wimbledon Hornets was offered an endless supply of free tobacco if he completed the task before his leg had mended. Curiously enough, when the RFU later launched its crusade against covert profession-alism, they declined to investigate whether Manton had thereby infringed his amateur status.

There were a number of differences between the laws drawn up by the RFU and the code practised at Rugby School at that time, chief among them the abolition of hacking and tripping. The somewhat barbarous practice of being permitted to scythe away at an opponent's shins may well have accounted for Manton's broken leg, and by doing away with it, the RFU increased the popularity of a game that by then was expanding rapidly throughout the Empire. It was eventually, albeit not immediately, abolished at Rugby School as well.

Another change was to the offside law, to more or less what it is today, i.e. bafflingly grey, and largely down to the referee's interpretation. However, there was no arguing with the ref in 1871, if for no other reason than the ref didn't exist. The captains of the two opposing sides were appointed sole arbiters of all disputes, in which case the most miraculous thing about rugby football in those days was that any match ever got finished. Try to imagine, if you can, a Tri-Nations international between New Zealand and South Africa without a referee. It would be like *Rollerball*.

Mostly, in a game that was so static that players could have taken the field after a five-course dinner without being too far off the pace, with prolonged rucks and mauls and virtually no passing or running, there was precious little to promote excitable disagreement, and all games were decided by kicks. If anyone did anything remotely revolutionary, such as touching down behind the opposition's line (called a 'run-in') it still didn't count unless the ball was goaled from a mark in line with the touch down.

Some idea of the turgid nature of the game can be gleaned from the scrummage law. If a player in possession was held or tackled, he had to shout 'Down!' and place the ball on the ground. A scrum was then formed, from which both sides strove to get the ball upfield by means of shoving and heaving. As handling wasn't allowed, anyone outside the scrum could have nipped off for a meat pie and a mug of tea without being seriously missed. One theory about Manton's thought processes as he lay back with his fractured tibia, was that he was so keen to get back playing again that he made sure that a broken leg was no great handicap when it came to taking part in a game of rugby.

The new RFU rules were not ready when Scotland played England in the first international at Raeburn Place in 1871, so it's anyone's guess how Scotland came to win the game, a twenty per side match watched by 4000. With the captains having to agree on everything, it is entirely possible that Scotland's skipper might have managed to get England's to agree on the legality of their winning score by the simple expedient of producing a claymore from his shorts. But in the event of a complete impasse, as in this case, decisions were taken by umpires. On this occasion it was Dr H.H. Almond, later headmaster at Loretto. In later years, Almond explained his philosophy on contested decisions. 'When an umpire is in doubt, I think he is justified in deciding against the side which makes the most noise. They are probably in the wrong.'

It is almost impossible to comprehend how a game as complex and physical as rugby, even in its nineteenth-century form, could have been played for so long without a referee. It was, in fact, ten years before decision-making went to neutral arbitration, in the form of two umpires and a referee. All three officials remained off the field, and if the two umpires failed to agree over a decision, the referee got the casting vote. It wasn't until 1885 that referees were issued with whistles. Somewhat bizarrely, the umpires were provided with sticks (later flags), which they raised when appealed to by one of the captains.

That, incidentally, was the same year as seven-a-side rugby first began, introduced by a Melrose butcher by the name of Ned Haig. It was not a question, however, of Haig being some kind of early visionary. The clubs involved were all strapped for cash, so they held a meeting and decided to cut down on the number of players to defray expenses. They also made it a knockout competition, and it was pronounced a great – albeit accidental – success. This innovation survives today. The Middlesex Sevens may no longer produce the excitement they once did at Twickenham, but there is now a world sevens national circuit.

In 1875 the game became a touch more enterprising when the fourth Varsity Match, a contest which survives to this day and has provided many internationals for all the major rugby-playing countries, was played with fifteen per side. The following year the extra space was utilised by a change in the ruck and maul rules; the ball had now to be released in the tackle. In 1877, for the first England–Ireland international, the game became even bolder when one of three defending backs went up to link with the half backs, and thus became the game's first threequarter. By 1881, this had expanded to a full trio of threequarters, and the following year, Cardiff developed the four threequarter system. Between 1879 and 1882, at Oxford University, Harry Vassall and Alan Rotherham developed a style of play with inter-passing between forwards and backs. The ball was now heeled from the scrummage so that the backs could run with it, but just as rugby was beginning to get a dangerous reputation for enlightenment, order was restored by the Scots and English getting involved in a game-splitting argument.

Ironically, after somehow managing to remain on speaking terms during all those years without a referee, it was a disagreement over a refereeing decision during the 1884 international match which started it all off. You were, in those days, allowed to throw or pass the ball backwards, but not to knock or hack it back, and when one of the Scots knocked back towards his own line, an Englishman nipped in to score the winning try. It sounds like the first recorded instance of playing advantage, but the Scots complained that the referee – an Irishman – should have halted the game with a penalty. England claimed, with a degree of reasonableness that was slightly out of character, that the Scots should not benefit from their own offence and that, in any event, the referee had made his decision in their favour and that was that.

'Let's refer it to arbitration,' said the Scots. 'Certainly,' said England, 'we'll ask the RFU to sort it out.' 'The RFU?' said the Scots, justifiably regarding the likelihood of a ruling in their favour as the rough equivalent of William Wallace receiving a small fine and a fortnight's probation from Edward I. 'Stuff that.' Or words to that effect. And that was the last time they spoke to each other for the next twelve months.

After the cancellation of the 1885 fixture, the Scots made the gesture of agreeing to play in 1886, on condition that England joined Scotland, Wales and Ireland on the home nations International Board on equal terms. England agreed to give the matter careful thought, although the mere notion of being regarded as equals to the Celtic nations must have had the RFU on tranquillisers for several weeks. Needless to say, England were still thinking about it two years later, by which time the Scots were not the only ones who had had enough. By 1888 and 1889 the stand off involved Wales and Ireland as well, and there was no England match against any home union in those two years.

Finally, in 1890, the year it was agreed that rugby's close time would be from 1 May to 31 August, England agreed to go to arbitration, which was considerably less of a surprise than Scotland, Ireland and Wales agreeing to the make-up of the tribunal, which, to all intents and purposes, was the rugby equivalent of an O.J. Simpson jury. They hadn't a hope of getting anything out of two English lords and an FA official with, believe it or not, the initials F.A. And FA is what they got. Lord Kingsburgh, the Lord Justice Clerk and Major F.A. Marindin, president of the Football Association, ruled that while all men might be equal in the eyes of the law, the law as applied to rugby football meant that England were more equal than the rest. They decreed that the vastly higher number of clubs in England should allow them more votes, and proposed six seats on the International Board for them, and two each for the Scots, Irish and Welsh. However reluctant the Celts might have been to tug the forelock, tug it they did.

The settlement effectively meant that England were allowed to dominate world rugby until the 1950s, especially as the RFU were not the least bit inclined to recognise the rise of the southern hemisphere nations, New Zealand, South Africa and Australia, by offering them anything as radical as voting rights; far better they were affiliated to the RFU! Despite giving up a couple of seats in 1911, the RFU monopoly enabled them to keep the Tri-Nations waiting until 1948 before agreeing to admit them on to the International Board, and it was not until 1958 that the southern hemisphere were granted the same number of seats – by this time, two – as the four home nations. France didn't get on until 1978.

Having neatly established the framework to dominate world rugby, the RFU were not the kind of body to tolerate any insubordination in the ranks – even their own – and it was at the start of 1890s that they took the high moral ground in a crusade that was to leave them comfortably the weakest side of the four home nations. Boot money was the reason, or to be more accurate, pocket money. It was, needless to say, common practice for players to remove all valuables from their belongings before going out to play, but up in the north of the country, players were returning to the dressing room to find that valuables had been put *into* their pockets rather than taken out – usually in the form of a nice crisp ten-bob note. It was all very different down south, where the players tended to be from the upper classes, but in Lancashire and Yorkshire, half a day off work in the textile mill left a significant hole in the pocket.

Rugby was popular enough in the north for the clubs to be raking in decent gate money, and if some of it found its way back to the players by way of lost wage compensation, this seemed fair enough. However, the RFU didn't quite see it that way, and continued not to for the thick end of another century. Less than twenty years ago, Leicester, who now pay out small fortunes in wages and bonuses, operated a policy of refusing to re-supply their players with a pair of shorts unless there was proof that they'd been ripped on the field of play.

Ninety years earlier, the RFU began to get wind of these player payments and eventually there was a direct charge levelled against one of the Yorkshire clubs by the union of Cumberland. A committee was set up to investigate, but none of the northern clubs felt too threatened; theirs was the player power-base of the English game, and they didn't think that the RFU would be too keen on a confrontation. They also let it be known that any adverse decision would not be taken lying down. However, RFU committee members have always been instantly recognisable by gunshot wounds in both feet, and after an official inquiry held at Preston, the guilty club was suspended. The northern clubs were not happy, not least because they had been perfectly open about compensating players for lost time at work, and pointing out that in any event the rules of rugby had not been framed with amateurism in mind. In other words, what they were doing was not illegal.

A general meeting was called, at which RFU officials met a northern club delegation who put their case for broken-time payments. The outcome, not surprisingly given the number of votes cast by southern clubs stuffed with lords, earls and other assorted gentry, was victory for the Establishment. Not long afterwards, Yorkshire's proposal that RFU annual meetings should alternate between north and south failed to gain the necessary 66 per cent majority, and resentment continued to smoulder.

By 1892, there was little sign of a change up north and, in fact, it had grown from compensation payments to what amounted to a flourishing transfer market, from which sprung the first player suspensions. Two Welsh brothers, Evan and David James, left their home in Swansea to join Broughton Rangers in Lancashire. Swansea claimed that the reason they'd left was because the club had refused their demand to be paid £1.10s. per week. They were both suspended.

By September 1893 the whole business came closer to boiling point when an RFU meeting was held at the Westminster Palace Hotel to consider a proposal that broken-time payments be made legal. Delegates from the north came down in two special trains to make sure of maximum representation, a plan that went slightly awry when many of them – unused to the bright lights of London – got themselves lost and never made it to the meeting. Furthermore, the RFU had worked a nice little flanker by granting voting rights to every college at Oxford and Cambridge, instead of one each to the two universities. On top of that H.E. Steed of Lennox FC had gathered 120 proxy votes. It was no contest. The Establishment won by 282 votes to 136, and immediately set about forming new laws to stamp out any hint of professionalism. In the league table of fanatical crusades, it was on a par with Joseph McCarthy rooting out imaginary communists in America in the 1950s.

The new laws were passed on 19 September, 1895, but by this time twenty-two northern clubs had already met at the Mitre Hotel, Leeds, where the decision was taken to form the Northern Football Union and resign from the RFU. They followed the broken-time payment principle for the next three years, then came out in favour of unrestricted professionalism, subject to the stipulation, later removed, that a player must have some kind of additional employment. (The RFU had other serious matters to deal with. In 1897, a ruling from the RFU declared that 'an injured player, who has retired from the game and stands on the touchline, can tackle a player provided he is not off-side'!)

The consequence of all this was the destruction of the most powerful county in the game, Yorkshire, and a massive reduction in strength of the second strongest, Lancashire. And for the next two decades England were left emasculated on the field. From a base of 481 clubs in 1893, it dipped to 244 clubs, and not until 1924/25 did the numbers climb back up to pre-split levels. It was a classic own goal. But for the RFU zealots going about their business like Peter Cushing in Transylvania, we'd probably never have heard of Eddie Waring. Now there's a thought.

CHAPTER 4

MULLOCK AND THE MONKEY

WELSH RUGBY: not so much a game, as a holy experience. In Wales, the red No. 10 jersey has the same religious significance as the Shroud of Turin, and in the maternity wards of the Principality, it is not difficult to conjure up an image of the midwife assuming the role of scrum half, spinning the new arrival across the room with a deft reverse pass, and into the arms of the proud father. 'I think we'll call him Barry, Phil, John, Gareth, Gerald, Carwyn . . .'

The actual invention of the reverse pass is widely credited to one of the stars of the famous 1905 side, Dickie Owen, who employed it to start the movement which led to the winning try against the All Blacks. Between 1900 and 1911 the Welsh were far and away the dominant country of the four home unions, with only Scotland providing a regular threat. In that period Wales lost only seven of forty-three games, and were more or less invincible at home, being beaten only by South Africa at Swansea in 1906.

The beginnings, though, were humble. Before this golden twelve-year era, which produced no less than seven Triple Crowns, Wales had won only sixteen internationals out of forty-six, and afterwards, until the 1950s in fact, they once again reverted into a long period of hopelessness, during which time – heavenly bread though it might have been – the Welsh dragon barely breathed enough fire to make a decent round of toast. Rugby had no particularly fierce grip on the nation until a meeting of the South Wales Football Club (who later changed their title to Union) at the Cardiff Arms Hotel on 23 October, 1877, in which it was decided to institute a Challenge Cup, open to any club subscribing a fee of two guineas. It gave rugby in the Principality a serious kick-start, igniting local rivalries between the likes of Newport and Cardiff, and Swansea and Llanelli. It was not until later – when the national team's identity was forged via a scarlet jersey and the Prince of Wales feathers – that the primary source of Welsh pleasure on the rugby field switched from internecine warfare to sticking it up the English.

The cup competition was something of a fly-by-the-seat-of-the-pants operation in that first year, and the decidedly basic lines of communication meant that Cardiff were only told the day before that their tie with Carmarthen had been switched from Neath to Swansea. They were not able to contact all their senior players in time, and duly lost with a below strength team. Newport were the first winners in 1878. The following year there was something of a farce when the whole competition ground to halt while Swansea and Neath were involved in a first-round tie that showed little sign of being resolved before the turn of the century. After five replays, and six draws in total, both sides – without so much as a penalty shoot-out – were unceremoniously kicked out in an attempt to get the competition moving.

Local rivalry was so intense in that period, that the rule stating that teams had to be made up of bona fide residents was seldom adhered to, and regular accusations were made of importing players from well beyond the stipulated twelve-mile radius. Some at least made a half-hearted attempt to comply with the regulations, even if it amounted to no more than staying with a cousin or an uncle on a Friday night.

There were also several cases of teams taking the game far too seriously (by employing underhand tactics such as training) and a prop forward who broke into anything resembling a trot was regarded as having breached the game's unwritten etiquette. In those early amateur days, if you arrived for a 3 p.m. kick-off after clocking-off the 6 a.m.–2 p.m. shift at the local steelworks, with only just enough time to struggle out of your overalls into your playing gear, you were regarded as a decent chap who played the game in the proper spirit.

The game in Wales, unlike England, was almost exclusively working class and, with the accent more on winning than on playing the game, was perceived by the RFU as a major threat to their own inflexible guidelines on what constituted commercialisation and professionalism. Even some of the Welsh administrators shared this view, and at the SWFC annual meeting in 1883, Neath's Tom Williams proposed that the cup competition be dropped. Williams argued, with stunningly perverse logic, that as the cup had achieved its objective of getting people interested in rugby, it was of no further use. Work that one out, if you can.

Mind you, interest in the competition had declined in any case to the point where only seven teams had entered in 1885–86, and it was thus decided that the following year would be the last. It was brought back in 1889, but only for second XVs and junior clubs, and even this was discontinued eight years later. However, the long-term future of Welsh rugby had already been assured – not least because of a population explosion which brought more than 200,000 extra people into Glamorgan in the last two decades of the nineteenth century. The coalfields of South Wales were booming, as were the ports of Newport, Cardiff and Swansea.

A boom time in any sport normally co-incides with having a superstar, and the Barry John of his day was undoubtedly Arthur Gould, known as 'the Monkey' for his schoolboy habit of shinning up trees. Not only did he become Wales's first legendary player, but he also has serious claims to be known as the first-ever rugby icon.

He was blindingly fast for a player of that era, able to run 100 yards in 10.2 seconds, and he made his mark with Newport on his debut at the age of sixteen when he was selected as emergency full back and scored two tries against Weston-Super-Mare. He played most of his rugby as a threequarter, although his first cap for Wales – in 1885 – was also at full back. Gould's employment as a public works contractor involved travelling all round the country, which accounted for the fact that he clocked up more than 4000 miles by train in 1885–86, playing for Southampton Trojans, London Welsh, Hampshire, Middlesex, South Wales and, latterly, Richmond. He was also something of a C.B. Fry, having been Midland Counties hurdles champion, and winning over £1000 in foot races. One Whit Monday, at the Newport Athletic Club, Gould won the open sprint, the hurdles, the 120 yards and the high jump.

He was also being considered for the high jump, at least metaphorically, by the RFU. Gould's early flirtations with professionalism began – one year after assuming the captaincy of Wales against Ireland – when he was honoured at a concert at the Albert Hall (the one in Newport) during which he was presented with a cheque for fifty guineas and what was described as a 'handsomely chased' gold ring. The gimlet eyes of the RFU were already glinting in his direction when Gould disappeared from rugby for eighteen months, assigned to the West Indies with his elder brother Bob on water and bridge project contract work. On his return he played for Newport, whose success that year was marked by each team member receiving a gold watch – the money raised by public subscription – and £5 per man from a magazine known as *Pearson's Monthly*. Gould's own commercial endorsements included selling match boxes with his face on them. He had a keen eye for a nice little earner – an Arthur Daley as well as an Arthur Gould.

Newport played far more games outside Wales than the other three big clubs in the Principality, although the eyes of the rest of the country were on them for more than just their playing skills. Not to put too fine a point on it, they were widely regarded as closet professionals. For one thing, horror of horrors, they possessed their own gymnasium – thus infringing rugby's great amateur ethos of no player ever taking the field in that unsporting condition known as fully fit. Not only that, Newport also exercised a degree of control over their players' off the field activities that was virtually unknown at the time, including restrictions on their alcoholic consumption. Even as late as the amateur 1990s there were senior rugby clubs all over Britain who would have lost all their players had they attempted to impose anything quite so radical. A rugby player restricting himself to less than ten pints on a Friday night would have been regarded as dangerously semi-professional.

By 1896 Gould's legion of admirers wanted to grant him a testimonial, which set off a palpitation attack at the RFU the like of which had not been seen since the northern clubs broken-time payment row. Wales wanted to give Gould a house but whether this was a country mansion in Carmarthen or a humble mid-terrace with an outside privy in a bleak mining valley, the RFU were having none of it. The RFU laws had been redrafted in 1895 forbidding the giving or receiving of any money or testimonial, or medal or prize, without the authority of the Rugby Union. A note was added that this was not meant to apply to a wedding present. Having already ruled that no monetary testimonial would be permitted, they now adjudicated that a house could easily be sold, and that Gould was effectively taking the feathers from the Welsh jersey for his own nest. Wales, having temporarily withdrawn from the four nations International Board, knew that they were in trouble when Scotland sided with the auld enemy, England, over the issue, and the chastened Welsh not only withdrew their cash offer of £50 towards the Gould testimonial, they also refused to sanction any presentation not approved by the IB.

Nonetheless, on Easter Monday 1897, at Newport's Drill Hall, Gould was given a house, and in September of that year the RFU, along with the other members of the IB, decreed that he had professionalised himself. With all sorts of decrees flying around, along the lines of blackballing any side either playing with him or against him, Gould solved the problem himself by announcing that he would not play again.

In 1892 Gould had demonstrated his power over his public by coming to the rescue of English referee Hodgson after he disallowed a penalty by Evan James against Scotland. It is claimed the official only made the safety of Swansea's Mackworth Hotel because he was accompanied by Gould. When the match committee met to chose the team for the Irish game, they formally regretted the behaviour of the Swansea crowd, but requested that the RFU 'appoint competent men to act as referees in international matches'.

It was not a safe time for referees. Later that year an official was attacked after awarding Swansea a dropped goal then disallowing it following Cardiff protests. Newspaper offices were attacked for printing the correct score. Stones thrown at the referee cost one bystander the sight of an eye. Swansea's appeal to the WFU was upheld; the committee reversed the referee's decision on the grounds that he should not have changed his mind. In February the following year, after a Special General Meeting and much East–West Wales bad feeling, the original position was restored; a few months later the Welsh Referees Society was formed.

Gould could do no wrong. One of his finest moments on the field came in 1893 when Wales met England at the Arms Park in Cardiff in the middle of a snap so cold that eighteen tons of coal were consumed in 500 braziers to ensure that the pitch was fit for play. In front of 20,000 spectators England led 7–0 at half-time and, with Marshall scoring their second try shortly after the break, it looked all over. However, Gould then scored two tries to bring Wales right back into the game and, with time almost up, Wales were awarded a potentially match-winning penalty on the 25 and close to the touchline. Gould called up Bancroft for the kick, first electing to hold the ball himself on a pitch so hard that nothing but a blow torch would have made a big enough indentation for placing it, but on second thoughts opting for a drop kick instead. Gould recalled five years later that 'with a grand kick, Bancroft dropped the ball over the centre of the bar.' Whatever plans

Gould might have had for a hot shower after the game had to be abandoned when the pitch was invaded, and he was carried shoulder high from the stadium and straight to the Angel Hotel across the road. Ironically, had the RFU adopted new scoring values proposed by Wales earlier that year, the game would have been drawn 14–14.

Gould had retired before Wales ruled the four-nations roost in the early part of the twentieth century, and while seventy years later it was the glittering backline talent of the likes of Barry John, Gareth Edwards, JPR, Gerald Davies and Phil Bennett which bewildered the opposition, in this era it was brute strength up front which formed their power-base. Up until then, Wales had been regarded as a soft touch in the forward battle, but with the mines and steelworks now churning out big, hard men, Wales forsook the sabre for the sledgehammer. The chimneys belching smoke over industrial South Wales in those days did not represent fly-half factories so much as conveyor belts for forwards.

There were still legendary figures behind the scrum, such as outside half Percy Bush, scrum half Dickie Owen, and the waiflike threequarter Billy Trew, but perhaps the most unusual thing about the Welsh team of that period is that their supporters were never quite sure which player would be first man out of the tunnel. The captaincy seems to have been a case of who fancied the job on the day, and in 1908 Wales won four matches with four different leaders. Willie Llewellyn, who led Wales to the 1905 Triple Crown, recalled: 'for two seasons, 1906/7 and 1907/8, we did not worry a great deal about captaincy, and virtually decided among ourselves as to which man would lead. He was the "boss" on the day, but there were no complicated preparations, and we did not like selectors or WRU committee men interfering with us or giving us orders as to what we should do in our matches. During the Golden Era, the team almost selected itself. We knew each other's play intimately and often times we recommended players to the selectors. We remembered the players of opposing countries and knew how to deal with them. We did not get excited before a match, but played with confidence, and everyone knew his job.'

The Newport influence on early Welsh rugby manifested itself in Richard Mullock, who belonged to a family of steam-powered printers (Henry Mullock & Son) of Commercial Street, and it was to him that J.B.G. Thomas dedicated his history of Welsh rugby, *The Men In Scarlet*. Mullock, secretary of the Newport Athletic Club from 1874, was more of an opportunist than a visionary, who saw the chance to take charge in Wales at a time when the SWFU was a weak, disorganised body, operating a fixture structure of clashes and conflicts that often left Welsh clubs below strength and disadvantaged in matches against English opposition.

Mullock organised a SWFU meeting at the Tenby Hotel in Swansea in March, 1880, which effectively marked the formation of the Welsh Rugby Union (or Welsh Football Union as it was known until 1934). At this meeting Mullock managed to secure a mandate to challenge England to an international match. At the time, this was the rough equivalent of the current England side receiving a challenge from the Old Boozeonians 3rd XV, and it received a sniffy response. The RFU recorded in their minutes that they had received a letter from 'a Mr R. Mullock of Newport, proposing a match with Wales' and it was finally agreed upon with the snooty post-cript '. . . after considerable discussion'. England had played nineteen internationals by then, losing only twice, to Scotland, and the scarlet jerseys chosen by Mr Mullock – previous representative teams under the SWFC had worn black vests with leeks across the chest – served merely to match the colour of Welsh faces as the English gave them a sound thrashing.

Mullock was pretty clearly a likeable chap with the inability to organise a piss-up in a brewery, and on the one occasion he managed to do so – literally – it was slightly unfortunate that he arranged it for his own Welsh team before that first international against England. Under Mullock's stewardship, the Welsh side changed in a nearby hostelry, and rumours had it that they kept the barman so busy that one or two players left the dressing room with boots on the wrong feet. The captaincy had been offered to C.P. Lewis, who declined on the grounds that Mullock's team did not represent the real strength of Welsh rugby. He was right, too, not least because it would have been slightly more reflective of the strength of Welsh rugby had they turned up with fifteen players, as opposed to thirteen. One of the missing men was J.E. Brooks of Pontypridd, who later recalled: 'It was mentioned to me that Treharne and I had been chosen to play for Wales against England in the first international. I had no definite instructions to play in that match, but I heard afterwards that I had been expected to play.'

The account of the day revealed that the missing two players were replaced by pulling out of the crowd 'two Varsity men with Welsh qualifications', although it is not known whether the Welsh qualification was then more rigorous than an ability to say 'Iechyd da' (pronounced yakidah)' in a New Zealand accent. Imagine queuing up for a pre-match hot dog at the Millennium Stadium and having the Welsh manager tap you on the shoulder saying, 'Fancy a game this afternoon, lads?' Perhaps the two men hauled off the terraces in 1881 were on the same wavelength as the rest of the team, and had prepared for the game in the saloon bar at the local pub.

This 1881 defeat gave rise to the first instance of what was to become a national pastime – Welsh rugby fans writing to the *Western Mail* to slate the selectors, or in this case, selector. If it was hard work humping coal for a living in the old mining days, it was even harder on the lumbar regions for a postman, who would come from work bent over like Quasimodo when Wales lost a game. One letter in the *Western Mail* that year demanded to know: 'Was this the official Welsh side, or a private team got up by Mr Mullock of Newport?'

A Mr Clarke, honorary secretary of the SWFU, responded:

'I beg to inform your correspondent that the team representing Wales was not selected by the committee of the SWFU, neither had they anything to do with it. As your correspondent assumes, Mr Mullock was one of the committee who selected the Welsh team, and will, no doubt, be pleased to give any information.'

Mr Mullock, not surprisingly, was not at all pleased to supply the information. He kept his quill dry, and his head well below the parapet, although his venture did at least have the effect of prompting the formation of the WFU – the SWFC having been disbanded at the Tenby Hotel meeting. The WFU was formed to put a halt to Mullock's private entrepreneurial activities, and he agreed to disband his private squad after being offered the post of WFU secretary. He was also appointed treasurer, which might have been a good idea but for Mullock's apparently chronic inability to add up. His balance sheets were less inclined in style to a neatly penned ledger than to scribble on the back of a fag packet. His first year in charge produced receipts of £96. 11s. 4d. and expenditure (largely on entertaining) of £215. 10s. 0d. One WFU representative, and another Newport man, Horace Lyne, described the accounts as being in a 'regular mess'.

Even on those rare occasions when he was able to announce a profit, Mullock had an unfortunate talent for coming across as a bit of a muddle-head, as was the case when the 1887 international against England at Stradey Park, Llanelli, in front of an 8000 crowd, yielded a surplus of £23. However, it should have been more. Because of poor weather and doubts about the state of the ground, Mullock had sent a telegram to St Helen's, Swansea, asking them about pitch conditions there, and rumours of a switch of venue caused several hundred spectators to turn up there instead.

When Mullock eventually resigned as treasurer, the committee voted him a retiring testimonial of a hundred guineas, and then took the eminently sensible decision to replace him as secretary as well with someone with a better grasp of balancing the books, removing the honorary from the title, and offering an annual salary of £50.

In 1893, a couple of weeks after the great Welsh frozen pitch triumph over England, Mullock resigned from the WFU committee, and his printing firm was declared bankrupt the same year. His next public appearance, in 1902, gave some indication of the hard times he had fallen on – he was sued in court for a debt of £3. He pleaded inability to pay on the grounds that he had been a commercial traveller for the previous two years, selling black and white drawings that earned him about £1 per month. Not surprisingly, he was having trouble supporting a wife and six children on this, and shortly afterwards he emigrated to Africa.

CHAPTER 5

RUGBY'S FUTURE ALL BLACK

IF YOU LISTEN TO CYNICS and Australians, New Zealand is the kind of place where people can still be found doing the hula-hoop in the queue for a Beverley Sisters concert, where the only thing liable to knock you down crossing a main road is a stray hump of tumbleweed, and where the millennium bug is not due to strike until 2040. However, if this beautiful and delightfully laid-back country is ahead of its time in anything, then it's rugby.

New Zealand also has more holes in its ozone layer than most places on the planet, and while the scientists can argue all they like about greenhouse gases and global warming, most rugby aficionados are firmly of the belief that the majority of those holes were made by Colin 'Pine Tree' Meads jumping at the line-out.

There are many examples of rugby union's near trance-like grip on the New Zealand people, foremost among them the punch-ups on the streets between rugby fanatics and the anti-apartheid lobby in the days when the New Zealand–South

Africa fixture was the All Blacks versus the No Blacks. I had my own first-hand experience of rugby fanaticism in New Zealand when the All Blacks' new rugby jersey for the 1999 World Cup – modestly entitled the 'strip of the century' – was unveiled live on their national TV. Up until that moment, the accolade of rugby union's strip of the century had largely been accorded to Erica Roe's half-time appearance at Twickenham in 1982, wearing what England's scrum half Steve Smith memorably described as Billy Beaumont's bum on her chest. But this ceremony, which was essentially to unveil nothing more than a higher-tech version of a black shirt, was given bigger media treatment than a royal wedding, and the new collarless shirt was the talk of the nation.

The reasons for rugby being accorded semi-religious status in New Zealand, even more so than in Wales, are not immediately obvious, although it clearly has something to do with the rugged nature of the country, and the big, hard, fit men it has produced from generations of working the land and the sheep farms. Wilson Whineray, one of the legendary All Black captains, said: 'In the early times, rugby football must have been an enormous help to the lonely rural folk living in a widely scattered community. We worked hard in those days, had little company, no telephones, no wireless. The Saturday get-together was very important to us.' In Australia, the country comes to a complete halt on one day of every year, for a horse race in Melbourne. In New Zealand, now that they have the wireless (which might come as news to some Australians) the same applies whenever their beloved All Blacks take the field.

As for the home unions, their cosy, staid and largely insular world was shaken for ever with the arrival of the first All Black touring teams at the start of the twentieth century. Here was a distant outpost of the Empire that had taken the game given to them by their colonial masters and turned it into a game of power and skill at which the British could only marvel.

The first touring sides to arrive on these shores were the Maoris, who might have raised an eyebrow or two at the complaints about fixture congestion in the modern professional era. In 1888/89 they played three or four times per week in an itinerary embracing seventy-four matches, winning forty-nine of them. Whether the opposition were more taken aback by the Maori rugby or having the opposition stick their tongues out at them is a moot point. Mind you, the Maoris themselves might have been a bit startled by the programme for their game against Oxford University in which the students whimsically – in deference to a side from the other side of the world – printed their names upside down. Those Maoris left a lasting legacy – the Haka. It was a Maori 'posture dance', although the rugby team kindly decided to perform it without the traditional spears, and it has become not only an All Black institution, but a rugby one as well.

The first great touring side from New Zealand, however, was the 1905 All Blacks, captained by Dave Gallaher, who forced the home countries to re-examine their thinking with a game based on speed, support and accuracy of pass. It was as big a culture shock to the rugby fraternity as the arrival of the horseless carriage to replace the pony and trap had been to society as a whole. It was similar to the culture shock experienced by the players and spectators at Wembley when England were thrashed by the Hungarians in 1953. The All Blacks won thirty-four of their thirty-five matches, their single defeat coming against Wales in Cardiff, by 3 points to 0. Such were the innovations and variations, that many of the spectators in this country thought they were watching a new game.

Gallaher, and his vice-captain Billy Stead, afterwards wrote a book entitled *The Complete Rugby Footballer* in which they outlined their philosophy: 'Each side, and each player on the side, must have their recognised ruses . . . a ruse can seldom be tried more than once in a game, but every ruse has, as it were, a double edge. When you have cut with it one way, you can turn round and cut with it the other. You gain by the mystery you create and nothing has such a demoralising effect on a side as being beaten by these feints.'

The most obvious difference between the sides was the skill levels. In the home nations, players had a more or less one-dimensional job to do depending on their positions, while the All Black players were expected to be able to kick with both feet and pass with both hands. In short, what was viewed as special by home supporters was accepted as standard by their visitors. Among the innovations they brought with them was using a forward to throw in at the line-out, and employing one of the wing forwards to put the ball in at the scrum. The scrum half still collected from the heel, but the detached wing forward was always ready to spoil the opposition possession should they manage to steal the heel. By using angles and pressure points, the New Zealand pack overcame most of the eight-man scrummages they came up against.

They used codes and signals for planned moves, but the biggest difference of all was in what the British called a 'loose scrum', which they called a ruck. 'Our backs never go down and lie on the ball as they do in Britain,' wrote Gallaher, 'permitted as they are by the referees. In New Zealand, if a back does not get up immediately, he is penalised. We find that lying on the ball slows the game a great deal, particularly when the referee merely gives a scrum. Besides, this method of procedure is a fruitful cause of accidents.' Quite. Most of the accidents being caused by All Black studs forcibly removing parked opposition bodies from the scene.

Another major difference was the attitude towards forwards running with the ball, which was unheard of in Britain, where rugby more or less mirrored the class system. The forwards were, as it were, below stairs, fetching and carrying, while the backs represented the aristocracy. Even when the game in this country finally embraced specialised coaching and diet sheets, the primary role of a front-row forward was still to heave and shove, and I remember an international prop from one of the leading clubs of the 1980s being ribbed unmercifully in the bar afterwards over the fact that he'd scored a try. He'd only flopped over the line from about three yards out, but it was still – in the culture of the time – regarded as a fining offence.

The 1905 All Blacks, however, showed no such reticence when it came to initiating attacks from their pack, and they scored thirty-three tries directly from line-outs. This also marked them down as the first team to keep statistics. They seldom kicked, apart from relieving pressure inside their own 25, and while British sides employed the maul as a handy method of taking a breather, the All Blacks rucked in order to keep the ball alive. 'The ruck,' said Colin Meads, 'is born of a desire to get the ball for the backs.'

They also unveiled the hitherto unheard of tactic of missing out men in passing movements, which had the regular effect of bemusing home defences, who were used to seeing the ball passed from man to man like a bucket of water being ferried along the line at a fire. Gallaher wrote: 'Study the tactics of the old masters, then adapt them to the modern conditions. It is wonderful what a trifling chance will do in the way of furnishing a most complete alternative to an existing system of play. In many cases, the missing out of one man in the passing movement will throw the whole of the defensive machinery of the opposition out of gear.'

It is only comparatively recently that the British forward has shed the fond but revealing monicker of 'donkey', whereas, even in 1905, the All Blacks looked upon their own donkeys, as it were, as potential Derby horses. Gallaher/Stead again: 'We have noticed a shocking neglect in the choice of cultivation of the men in the front rank. The prevailing idea seems to be that . . . you put in this department all those men who are not thoroughly capable of any other task. Our principle is that every forward should be a potential back, and in the team that toured through Britain there was not a man in the pack who could not have fulfilled the duties of a back if emergency had demanded.'

They also brought with them the attacking full back, as opposed to the kind of traffic-policeman-on-point-duty style of No. 15 favoured over here, along with lines of running, drifting, scissors passes, attacking from kick-offs, and dummy runs without the ball. There was the reverse pass too, although in this instance there was encouraging evidence that some old British dogs were capable of learning new tricks, as it was employed during the movement leading to the Teddy Morgan try for Wales in the All Blacks' solitary defeat. It came at the end of tour, when the All Blacks were exhausted and weakened by injuries and, as Gallaher admitted, in an unusually negative frame of mind in their desire to go home with an unbeaten record.

The All Blacks' style was so incisive that, for the opposition, it was a bit like taking on a medieval lancer with a cocktail stick. It was not until their seventh game that the tourists' line was breached, although Durham, the champion English county from the previous season, still went down 16–3. The All Blacks responded with fifteen tries of their own in the next game against Hartlepool, and there were further avalanches in the following two matches against Northumberland and Gloucester. After the Gloucester game (44–0) one critic wrote: 'It was a triumph of mind plus matter over pluck and grit minus physique and the right conception.'

In the thirteenth game, the All Blacks had another severe fall from grace by conceding try number two on tour against the Midland Counties at Leicester, and around this time there was the first outbreak of what was to become a regular feature in northern versus southern hemisphere clashes, bleating over different interpretations of the laws. The All Blacks were restricted to an 11–0 margin over Surrey largely because the referee, Billy Williams, spent so much time blowing his whistle it was a wonder he wasn't stretchered off with a collapsed lung. 'A whistling fantasia', was how one visiting scribe saw it. Williams, though, of the London Society and later Twickenham Cabbage Page fame, claimed that the New

Zealanders were handling the ball out of the scrum when trying to screen it with their knees. And after the All Blacks had beaten Richmond 17-0, an England international, S. Reynolds, writing in the *Daily Mail*, complained: 'as the New Zealanders are such a really good side, they could leave out the obstructing and offside play, of which they are undoubtedly guilty.'

In match twenty, the first international, the All Blacks came close to defeat for the first time when Scotland were leading by a point with seven minutes remaining. However, two tries in the dying minutes preserved the tourists' record. Soon after came the Irish game, which the All Blacks won 15-0, a match missed by Gallaher because of an injury sustained at Inverleith. Stead's account suggests that Irish tactics have remained largely unchanged for the past century: 'They made the pace very hot indeed for the early part of the game. In the circumstances, we thought that the best thing to do would be to let them run about as much as they wanted and tire themselves out. We could bide our time.' The twenty-fourth match, against England, was one of the All Blacks' easiest. England had lost twelve of their previous fifteen internationals, and although 50,000 turned up at Crystal Palace, the tourists' winning margin of 15-0 could, in the opinion of most, have been at least doubled had the weather not been – a bit like England's play – intolerably wet.

Wales, though, were a different proposition in match twenty-eight, surprising the opposition firstly by packing down with only two men in the front row, and then opening them up with Owen's reverse pass to Pritchard, leading to Morgan's try near the corner. Deans claimed an equalising try for the All Blacks when he touched down right on the line after a tackle, but the referee, Scotland's John Dallas, who had scored a try in the Calcutta Cup victory two years earlier, awarded a scrum five instead. Even the Welsh players disagreed about whether it had been a fair score. Morgan thought it was, but Rhys Gabe, who made the tackle, thought not. Under 1905 regulations, a player brought down short of the line was not allowed to use his momentum to carry on over it, and Gabe said: 'I brought Deans down outside the try line. This is definite.'

Fair try or not, C.C. Reade, a New Zealand journalist, thought the result a fair one. 'The game was absolutely the finest I have seen in the history of rugby football. By the end of the match the play of the Welshmen became a revelation. They demoralised the New Zealanders with that deadly, persistent onslaught on the blind side. The development of that attack, swift as a knife thrust, was a creation of genius, and it exposed the weak spot in the Colonials' defence.' The other weak spot for New Zealand was their own overseas tour planning committee, who had not very cleverly arranged for them to embark on the Welsh leg of their trip when they were half knackered. Wales were comfortably the strongest of the four home nations at that time, and for them it was a bit like Rorke's Drift in reverse. The opposition were running short of fit personnel, with the Welsh queuing up to get at them.

Swansea went down 4–3 and Newport were beaten 6–3. On Boxing Day, it was Cardiff's turn and the gates were closed early on a full house of 40,000 who witnessed yet another tight affair. Cardiff, unbeaten at the time, led for much of the game, and it was only a horrible mistake by their skipper Percy Bush that led to the All Blacks scoring a try to pinch it 10–8.

When the All Blacks returned to Britain in 1924–25, they learned their lesson from 1905 in scheduling slightly fewer matches, and won all twenty-eight of them with a points tally of 654 scored, and 89 conceded. Persisting with the seven-man scrum, this time they found it far tougher against opponents who had improved their technique, and the roving loose forward was still being heavily penalised by home referees. As a result, the All Blacks saw only about 30 per cent of the ball on average in their matches, and their tactics and strategy had long passed their sell-by date. So how did they go one better than the 1905 side?

Firstly, their skills in possession were still a light year ahead of the opposition, and they were also fitter, faster and stronger than the earlier tourists. One of the main features of the tour was the relative closeness of the matches until the latter stages, at which point they turned up the burner against tired opponents. And if the backs had been at the heart of the 1905 side's success, this time it was the forwards who ran the game with their close support play and slick inter-passing. Not only did they handle like backs, the All Black forwards also possessed clever rugby brains. In Britain, by way of contrast, any flicker of activity in the cranial department tended to disqualify anyone from becoming a forward.

The star attraction was a nineteen-year-old Maori full back from Hawke's Bay, George Nepia, who was not allowed to tour South Africa four years later on racial grounds. Nepia played all twenty-eight matches and his impact was staggering, considering that he had never played full back before the tour. Denzil Batchelor wrote: 'He was between short and tall, and his thighs were like young tree trunks. His head was fit for the prow of a Viking Longship, with its passion-less, sculptured bronzed features and plume of blue-black hair. Behind the game he slunk from side to side like a black panther on the prowl.'

The tour took place in the middle of a highly successful period for English rugby, although this was not reflected in results against the tourists, who went through this leg of the trip with minimal inconvenience. Once again it was in Wales that they ran into the sternest opposition, and Newport gave them their hardest test in a game that finished 13–10. The full Welsh side, on the other hand, were thumped 19–0 at Swansea. With 50,000 locked into the ground, Wales proved to be difficult opponents only up until the moment the referee blew his whistle for the start of the game. By that time, no less than four balls had been rejected as unsuitable, starting with the Welsh captain, J. Wetter of Newport, objecting to the first one on the grounds that it was too hard. He also declined the replacement as it was 'not new', as he did ball number three, and Jock Richardson, the All Blacks' captain, took a dislike to the fourth. Wales, metaphorically speaking, did not play the actual game with the same amount of balls, and were muscled to a comprehensive defeat.

Llanelli did rather better in going down only 8–3, as perhaps was to be expected with the tourists having their usual period of rest and recuperation between fixtures – all of two days. King George V was in attendance at Twickenham as the Combined Services were seen off 25–3, and the only real threat now remaining to the All Blacks going home with a perfect record came from England. This time the royal presence in the committee box was the Prince of Wales, although in the atmosphere that prevailed before the kick-off, a Roman Emperor in a toga would have been more appropriate. A record crowd of 60,000 was crammed into the ground, the gates were closed half an hour before kick-off, and in the opening exchanges the two sides hit each other with everything – fists, mostly.

Len Corbett, acknowledged as the best giver and timer of a pass of his day, a county cricketer, and later a rugby and cricket correspondent of the *Sunday Times*, recalled: 'There is no doubt that both sides were keyed up to a pretty high pitch, and some indications of this were apparent in the first minutes of the game. Robust forward play, to use a polite term, was the feature of the opening phases. I prefer to call it plain rough housing. The referee, A.E. Freethy, found it necessary to issue a warning very early to both packs that he did not intend to allow the proceedings to degenerate into a free-for-all. His warning went unheeded, and when a scrummage was formed after seven minutes, something occurred which caused Mr Freethy to take the unprecedented action of sending a player off the field in an international match.'

And so Cyril Brownlie passed into history as the first-ever

player to be dismissed in an international match, and we are indebted to Len Corbett for telling us precisely why. Correction. Corbett, reporting in a manner which would nowadays have his sports editor foaming at the mouth, was apparently able to tell us no such thing. His report continued as follows: 'Unhappily, the player concerned was the magnificent All Black forward Cyril Brownlie.' Mean and moody, as well as magnificent it would seem, but Corbett then went blathering on about what a jolly fine chap the ref was. 'Mr Freethy was the ablest, fairest and firmest referee it was my experience to play under, and unfortunate and regrettable though this incident undoubtedly was' (er, what incident?) '. . . I have no reason to suppose that his judgement was at fault or his action was unjustified.' Why not? Corbett's final mysterious conclusion was: 'It is perhaps significant that Mr Freethy had refereed several of the All Blacks' previous matches.'

Corbett presumably failed to win that year's investigative journalist of the year award, and we would have been better informed, particularly as the game was more of a boxing match than a game of rugby, with a report from James J. Corbett. You would have thought one of the players could have shed more light on it, but the exact nature of Brownlie's crime was made no clearer in this account from the England captain that day, W.W. Wakefield. 'Instead of packing in the centre of our three man front row, which naturally would have always given us the loose head, they kept trying to work the loose head for themselves,' said Wakefield, 'which meant that our far prop overlapped into thin air. Well, we weren't going to have that.

'Reg Edwards, the England prop, had played for his club Newport against the tourists and he had had a pretty tense struggle over this matter of the loose head, so I think a few old scores were being paid off. But it was quite wrong to blame Reg Edwards for what happened at Twickenham.' Why? W.W. doesn't tell us.

He goes on: 'The prime cause of the trouble was the lack

of the law to define a front row, and then, when things started to get out of hand, Albert Freethy, the referee, said he would send off the next player he saw doing anything wrong. Well the next player happened to be Cyril Brownlie, and off he went.'

But what for? Biting an ear? Grabbing someone by the unmentionables? Presumably the ref sent Cyril on his way with something more specific than: 'I have seen you doing something wrong, Mr Brownlie. Pray leave us, if you would be so kind.' One appreciates that this was in the days before press conferences and seventeen different angles of Sky replays, but it is still curious that there appears to be no definitive version of the precise nature of Cyril's offence.

Wakefield shed no further light other than to point out that Brownlie was a Hawke's Bay player, and that it was his custom to step in to 'take the part of another All Black player from the same province whenever there was a bit of trouble'. But one thing Wakefield was sure of, apparently, is that it did England no favours.

'I have always felt that the sending-off of Brownlie cost us the game. It affected the England team far more than the All Blacks, who played above themselves. We had already scored one try from a long, controlled dribble by the forwards and we were about to score another when Brownlie was sent off.' The final score was 17–11, England's rally from a 14-point deficit not quite enough.

The one thing we do know from the incident is that the Reg Edwards referred to was never chosen for England again, although it was never made clear whether it was for something unsavoury he might have been involved in that afternoon. We also know that Brownlie made it back home to New Zealand, unlike another All Black who earned notoriety in Britain on Ian Kirkpatrick's 1972/73 tour, Keith Murdoch.

The All Black prop was sent home alone for chinning a bouncer outside the Angel Hotel in Cardiff following the international against Wales, but with reporters gathered on the tarmac to greet him, Murdoch failed to alight from the aircraft. It was thought that he had got off in Australia and found his way to some remote corner of the outback. Several years later, the doyen of New Zealand journalists, T.P. McLean, tracked him down to a tiny airfield in the middle of the Australian outback. Before McLean could speak, Murdoch picked up a monkey-wrench spanner and invited him to return to the light aircraft that had just brought him the last few hundred miles. McLean decided to live to fight another day and left without a word, never mind an exclusive interview. Clearly, one or two areas of All Black history remain all grey.

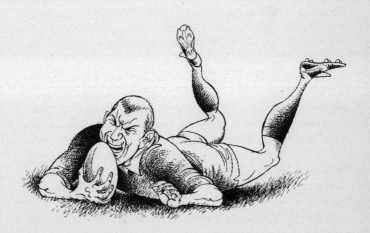

CHAPTER 6

ENGLAND CLOSE DOOR TO LOO-TIME PAYMENTS

Among the RFU's lesser known achievements is to have indirectly added, albeit not quite as comprehensively as Field Marshal Haig, to the English death toll in the 1914–18 Great War. Shortly after hostilities broke, they personally contacted every player urging them to sign up, and while it was nothing like as alluring an invitation as the General Kitchener posters, it was enough to sway many impressionable young men in those early war years of voluntary conscription. One assumes the RFU remained true to their principles in declining to pay any funeral expenses, just in case it left anyone tainted for life as a posthumous professional.

The war also had a not insignificant effect on ever-hardening RFU attitudes towards closet professionalism, in that the young men who survived the carnage came home with a determination to enjoy life to the full, without the pervading influence of money or inducements, and that included playing rugby. The ethos of playing the game for the game's sake was reinforced by their ghastly experiences in the trenches, and the bayonets against professionalism remained firmly fixed in the RFU committee rooms.

Ironically, after the great broken-time divide, the next dispute over money involved the Scots accusing England of encouraging the spread of professionalism because the RFU, without reference to the other Unions, had agreed to pay three shillings a day expenses to the touring Australian side of 1908/09. Scotland dug in their heels by refusing to pay – and in consequence play – the tourists. Only the truly cynical could have viewed this as anything other than a spirited defence of the game's morals, as opposed, shall we say, to another example of Scots turning pale at the prospect of spending money. England, however, unlike one or two of their early treasurers, had been doing their sums properly, realising that three bob a day was cheap at half the price for a visit from a major touring team. The 1905 All Blacks had made the turnstiles click as never before and, armed with the loot from that visit, invitations went out to the two other southern hemisphere giants, South Africa and Australia.

England were clearly more intent on getting the tourists into the country than formulating any serious plans to actually beat them. They still showed little inclination to abandon or modify a selection policy centred largely around the class system. The split with the northern clubs had emphasised that the Establishment game in England was strictly for the toffs, and that it was all very well having a fancy side-step or a thunderous boot, but any player who didn't know how to wear a monocle properly, or didn't get their names on to the invitation lists for enough high society balls and banquets, went straight to the back of the queue.

The New Zealand captain, Gallaher, wrote after the 1905 tour: 'One cannot help thinking that England might have picked a stronger side for their international match against us. By the time of the game we had had considerable experience of the class of player to be found in the towns and shires, and we certainly did not think that the fifteen who were put up against us at the Crystal Palace were fully representative of the best to be found in the country.'

Whether or not the England selectors chose their 1909 side to play Australia after exhaustive scrutiny of all the available talent, or chose their XV with a blindfold, pin and a copy of *Burke's Peerage*, they lost the match 9–3 in what was to be the last-ever international played on the Rectory Field at Blackheath. Twickenham was just around the corner, and it was only a delay in building the spectator stands there which took the match against Scotland that year to the Richmond Athletic Club.

The game was very nearly cancelled because the Scots were still banging on about England paying expenses to Australia, but after a last-minute truce a crowd of 20,000 – including the Prince of Wales – saw Scotland win 18–8. It was, however, a match that came to be remembered less for the quality of rugby, which all agreed was pretty ordinary, than for the quality of the referee, which he himself agreed was even worse than ordinary. It was the only international ever refereed by the former Welsh rugby player Gwyn Nicholls, which came as a relief not only to the rugby-playing fraternity in general, but also, in all probability, to Nicholls himself. He left the field with the immortal comment: 'Wasn't I awful?'

That was in March 1909, and on 2 October Twickenham was ready to stage its first club match, Harlequins v Richmond. G.V. Carey of Quins kicked off, as he did to mark the opening of the Stoop Memorial Ground fifty years later, by which time, one imagines, it was bit like watching Gene Sarazen hitting off at the age of ninety-seven as honorary starter of the US Masters Golf tournament at Augusta. After that first game, won by Harlequins 14–10, one journalist wrote, with some degree of prescience: 'Twickenham will, in the course of time, become a real live rugby centre; it is a district that is growing, and the game played in such an entertaining way as it is by the Harlequins will make rugby the recreation and sport of the young men of the neighbourhood.'

The first international match at Twickenham was on 15 January, 1910, when England beat Wales (11–6) for the first time for twelve years. Twickenham, in fact, probably became the first international bogey ground, given that Wales had to wait until 1933 for their first victory there. The first kick-off at Twickenham was delayed by fifteen minutes because of traffic congestion (which only goes to prove that some things in the game never change) and England marked the occasion by scoring a try inside the first sixty seconds. Wales kicked off, Adrian Stoop caught it and, as if determined to christen the new turf with the spirit of adventure, galloped away upfield instead of taking the customary option of hoofing into touch. A loose scrum ensued, England won the ball again, and spun it across the back line for Frederick Chapman, regarded as the greatest exponent of the side-step in his time, to score in the corner. As well as claiming the first international try at Twickenham, Chapman also kicked the first penalty and conversion at this new home of rugby.

It is not hard to imagine the sense of anticipation in the crowd for England's second international there against Ireland a month later, but this time it was more in keeping with Twickenham's later reputation as one of the more staid international venues, with neither side managing – or even threatening – a single point. It cost England the first grand slam (1910 was the first year all four home countries had played France) as they went on to clinch their first championship since the breakaway eighteen years earlier with a 14–5 victory over Scotland at Inverleith. It was on the morning of this Calcutta Cup that the International Board met and stated: 'It was desirable . . . where touch-judges were appointed that they should report cases of foul or unfair play to the referee.' That law entered the statute books in 1980!

That first match against Wales netted the RFU a profit of £2000 – a sizeable return on their investment after Billy Williams, a well-known player and referee, had advised them to purchase ten and a half acres of market garden at

Twickenham for the sum of £5572.12s.6d. Hence the place coming to be known as Billy Williams' Cabbage Patch – the only known association between an England team and a vegetable until the *Sun* newspaper awarded the England footballers the honorary title of 'turnips' several decades later.

Having previously led a somewhat nomadic existence, with homes at Kennington Oval, Crystal Palace, Blackheath, Richmond and a variety of provincial grounds, England moved full time into their new HQ and, once settled in, started developing it into rugby's premier stadium. The first two stands, renamed from A and B to East and West, housed 3000 spectators each, there was terracing for 7000 at the South end, and additional accommodation for 24,000 more elsewhere around the ground. Twickenham made a brief return to its agricultural roots when it was used for grazing cattle and sheep during the First World War, and in the Second World War it had a variety of uses, including allotments (more cabbages) and as a Civil Defence base. The West car park, which nowadays conjures up images of canapés and champagne being consumed from the back of Land Rovers, was used as a coal dump, and in 1944 the West Stand was damaged by a particularly nasty up and under, a V2 rocket bomb.

By 1921, another seven acres of land were acquired on the west side, and the 1924 Calcutta Cup match was witnessed by 43,000 spectators. The North Stand was completed the following year, followed by an upper deck addition for the East Stand, and a revamped West Stand – including new dressing rooms, baths, tea rooms, bars and offices – was unveiled for the 1931–32 season. Another two acres were purchased in 1934–35, for £2200, adjoining the North car park, but the RFU passed up an option on a further twenty-eight acres to the east side after their accountants advised them to keep a careful eye on their overdraft.

Twickenham's development coincided with England's first great playing era and the appearance of some of their finest players. It became the spiritual home of rugby, a bit like the

MCC at Lord's for cricket, and any developing club or country always looked first to Twickenham and the RFU for guidance. The modest custodians of the RFU, of course, were not slow in letting these countries (and indeed everyone else) know that they were looking in the right place.

> *To become (a Compleat Footballer) your budding centre should live with a rugby ball just as your would-be bowler should always have a cricket ball in his pocket, except of course in church.*
>
> E.H.D. SEWELL, Bedford School and Harlequins

By the Second World War, Twickenham was a vastly different place from the one that sprang up in 1910, as the Scots could testify since, on their first visit in 1911, they wandered around looking in vain for the main gate and finally had to settle for a rather undignified entrance through the allotments. In the same year, Douglas 'Daniel' Lambert made an indelible mark in the 37–0 thrashing of France, with 22 points from two tries, five conversions and two penalties.

England's first defeat at their new headquarters came in 1913, when they lost 9–3 against a powerful Springbok side, their solitary score coming from a try from Ronnie Poulton, a threequarter of outstanding natural talent. Poulton later changed his name to Poulton-Palmer (a condition of inheriting a fortune from his uncle) but he didn't live long enough to spend much of it; he was killed in the Great War. Seven of that season's team died in the conflict, as, in all, did twenty-six England internationals. Poulton-Palmer, who scored five tries for Oxford in the 1909 Varsity Match, and four more in his final match against France at Stade Colombes in 1914, was a ruggedly good-looking individual and was generally regarded as one of the game's first pin-ups. He was also thought of as a thoroughly good bloke and, after being killed at the age of twenty-five by a sniper's bullet in Belgium, his company captain, in the letter home to his family, wrote: 'when I went round the Company, as they stood to, at dawn, almost every man was crying.'

Another international who died is still remembered today in an annual memorial match between the East Midlands and the Barbarians at Northampton. This was Edgar Robert Mobbs, DSO who, on being refused a commission in August 1914, raised his own company of 250 sportsmen for the Northants Regiment. He rose to command his battalion with the rank of Lieutenant Colonel in April, 1916, and fell in action at Zillebeke in July, 1917. Mobbs was reputed to have led an attack into no-man's-land by booting a rugby ball ahead of him and chasing after it.

Yet despite the grievous culling of so many accomplished players, which of course applied to all the home nations, England enjoyed one of the most successful periods in their history in the 1920s, winning the Grand Slam in 1921, 1923, 1924 and 1928. That made it, either side of the war, six Slams in eleven seasons. In that postwar decade, England produced some of their most famous players – and characters – including C.A. Kershaw and W.J.A. Davies, who played together fourteen times at half back and never finished on the losing side. One of the great characters of that time was Carston Catcheside, who leapt (almost literally) into rugby folklore with a try in the 1924 French match at Twickenham, scored after a move that owed more to the 110 metres hurdles than a game of rugby. Just before half-time Catcheside found himself clear with only the French defender L. Pardo to beat, but with no way around (apart from into trouble or into touch) as Pardo crouched down in readiness for the tackle. However, he never laid a hand on Catcheside, who vaulted clear over the top of him, and swaggered in for the try that put England 9–0 ahead. Catcheside also went over the top with an expenses claim on a trip from Newcastle to London, submitting a train fare for £3. The gimlet-eyed RFU treasurer sent him a cheque for the actual fare, £2.19s.11d., but the penny also dropped for Catcheside, so to speak, when making his next claim to London on official England duty. This time he itemised it. 'Train fare: £2.19s.11d; use of toilet 1d.' He got his £3 that time.

Carston Catcheside won eight caps between 1924 and 1927, and earned his reputation as a bit of a wag in his first international trial match, after which, in an effort to impress upon those picking the team that he had done more than enough to warrant being chosen, he wrote his name over the bald head of one of the watching selectors. It worked, and he scored two tries on his debut against Wales in the 17–9 victory at Swansea in January 1924. He became a selector himself between 1936 and 1962, and presumably took the precaution, when his hair began to thin, of wearing a hat to all international trial matches. He was chairman of the England selection committee from 1951 to 1962, during which time no international dinner was complete without a top-table speech from him. 'Catchy', as he was known, always introduced himself as 'the whitest man in England', although what he meant by that no one seemed quite sure. Perhaps it had something to do with his expenses claims – putting in for only one visit to the toilet when, particularly for a journey as long as Newcastle to London, two might have been considered eminently reasonable.

However, while England produced colourful characters such as Catcheside behind the scrum in the 1920s, it was the forwards who provided most of the brickwork for England's success in that period – Tom Voyce, Dr Ronald Cove-Smith (who captained the 1924 Lions because of William Wakefield's unavailability), Geoff Conway (who won the Military Cross in the Great War, A.F. (later Sir Arthur) Blakiston and, of course, Wakefield, the man described by many as the greatest England forward of his or any other generation.

England actually made an inauspicious start after the Great

War, losing their first game back against Wales, 19–5, at St Helen's, Swansea. The team photograph for that match became a minor collector's item because W.M. Lowry of Birkenhead Park appears in it and was all ready to take the field when it was decided that the heavy rain and a muddy pitch was more suited to the talents of Harold Day of Leicester and the Army. The result doesn't seem to bear that out, but Lowry did win his cap two weeks later against France, in a match England won 8–3. That Welsh match was also the game which marked Wakefield's debut.

Wakefield also played a part in one of the strangest tries ever scored in an international, during the Grand Slam season of 1923 in the match against Wales. England scored within fifteen seconds, without a single Welshman touching the ball. Wakefield kicked off into a stiffish wind, and the ball blew back to Price, the Leicester forward, who attempted to drop a goal. It went wide, and in the belief that it was going to roll on over the dead ball line, the Welsh stopped. Price, however, was clearly an optimistic sort of chap (what sort of forward tries to drop a goal into the wind with his first touch in an international?) and was following up to touch down as the ball came to a halt an inch or two in goal.

Later that season, the last international played away from Twickenham for sixty-nine years took place at Welford Road, Leicester, England beating Ireland 23–5, and their next game also marked the end of a venue – Inverleith. England had an 8–6 win over the Scots, who had been hoping for a first Grand Slam of their own that afternoon. That was to go to England after an Easter Monday 12–3 victory over France in the Stade Colombes.

Next year, 1924, produced England's fifth Grand Slam, starting with two away wins in Swansea and Belfast, followed by home victories over the French and the Scots. It also marked England's sixth championship in ten seasons, including thirty-three wins out of forty. New Zealand and Scotland, winning their first Grand Slam, beat England in

1925 and the following year the Scots won at Twickenham for the first time, 17–9, in front of King George V. That was Wakefield's final appearance at Twickenham and his last as captain; injury kept him out of the first half of the 1927 championship and he retired at the end of that campaign after England had lost to France for the first time.

Until Wakefield's time, specialist forwards had been slow to develop, and it was not until the mid-20s that the International Board decreed that all scrums should consist of no more than three players in the front row. It is hard to imagine now, but sometimes a scrum took place with all eight forwards strung out in a line across the field. Likewise, at the line-out, they were only just sorting out a system of specialist jumpers and support jumpers (i.e. obstructors and lifters) and the duties of the back row were also more clearly defined, in terms of attacking and defensive roles.

> *He was grimy; his scrum cap was torn; and his jersey was split. His best friend wouldn't have recognized him. Then his scrum cap was torn off his head and I heard a shrill childish voice cry, "Look! Look! There's Daddy!" A thousand or more eyes turned and saw a little girl of about three sitting by her young mother. And the player, who was the terror of his opponents, looked up, his mouth parted in a loving smile. He waved his hand for one fleeting moment, and then dived at a man who had the ball under his arm. "Wakefield again!" ejaculated a man at my side. "Isn't he wonderful?"*
>
> F.B. DOUGLAS-HAMILTON on W.W. Wakefield, England captain

'Wakers', as he was invariably known, was educated at Sedbergh, and despite being a giant of a man for the era, he was also as quick as any back, and won a number of high-class races including the RAF quarter-mile championship. He was one of the first forwards to take defensive duties seriously, but was also a formidable opponent going forward, either with ball in hand, or on one of his celebrated charges with the ball at his feet. As a dribbler, he was almost in the Stanley Matthews class. He captained England thirteen times in thirty-one internationals, and had to decline invitations to captain two Lions tours, to South Africa in 1924 and New Zealand six years later, because of work commitments. He played cricket for the MCC, served in Parliament for forty years, and became Lord Wakefield of Kendal.

The other England innovator of the age had played before the Great War. Adrian Stoop, like Wakefield, was a member of Harlequins. While Wakefield developed forward play, Stoop was involved behind the scrum, with particular reference to the half backs. The 1905 All Blacks had a profound effect on his thinking, not just with their dodging and weaving, but also with their lines of running. After he finished playing, Stoop always watched Harlequins matches at Twickenham from the North Stand. Wakefield wrote of him:

Stoop had a profound influence on half-back play. All sorts of people tried all sorts of new ideas in midfield play almost throughout the 19th century, but the fact remains that when Adrian Stoop started playing first-class rugby the half-backs still took it in turns to play what we now call scrum-half and fly-half. He decided that it was important that there should be specialisation in those two positions.

Gallaher's All Blacks undoubtedly made a great impression on him, because English football was very much down in the dumps. The split between the North of England and the Union on the question of broken time payments meant that English rugby lost a vast number of players, including nearly all their best forwards. This meant England had to devise something else, and when the New Zealanders drove home the point in 1905, Stoop was encouraged to develop his ideas in a whole variety of ways.

Stoop was the first to see how quite subtle adjustments in the angles of run in midfield could produce really dramatic differences in opportunity for runners further out in the centre or on the wing. Stoop's reason for watching from the North Stand was to see if the Harlequins' midfield backs were running straight.

After Stoop came W.J.A. 'Dave' Davies. England's fly half before and after the First World War retired in 1923 with twenty-two caps and was never on a losing side in the championship. Davies's final game was in Paris – he must have had an understanding bride because he combined the weekend with his honeymoon – and his final touch on an international field was a dropped goal. With some newlywed brides being asked to double up on honeymoon with a game of rugby, it would have been his final touch of the weekend, full stop.

CHAPTER 7

THINKING WITH THEIR FEET

ALL RECENT RUGBY INTERNATIONALS at Murrayfield have been sponsored by the Royal Bank of Scotland and then Lloyds TSB, a mutually beneficial arrangement in this modern commercial era, but one which would have been quite unthinkable for the larger chunk of the twentieth century. In that period, linking Scottish rugby to anything as directly connected to money as a bank would have been the equivalent, in the wake of international cricket's recent trauma over match-fixing, of an England v Pakistan Test match being sponsored by Joe Coral; or, given the pharmaceutical connotations attached to cycling, the Tour de France sponsored by Boots.

While the RFU were the original vigilantes in the war against quasi-professionalism, the Scots took over the mantle of the game's moral custodians with a zeal and fervour that would have made one of William Wallace's pre-battle speeches look like a lecture to the Musselburgh Rotary Club. The other home unions were far from soft when it came to rigorous application of the amateur ethos, but to the Scots, it was as though Moses had suddenly popped up with an Eleventh Commandment. Some would argue that 'Thou Shalt Not Pay' was merely a natural by-product of the national characteristic, but in point of fact the Scottish Rugby Union's unbending attitude towards the merest whiff of commercialism was mostly down to the fact that there was nothing like the commercial pressure north of the border compared to the game in England and Wales. Scotland, as a result, installed themselves as the spiritual defenders of the amateur faith, and were not shy of drawing the claymore against England (something else which came quite naturally) when it came to arguments about keeping rugby whiter than white. Scotland's rugby union officials were not the only twentieth-century zealots, of course, but while it is not difficult to conjure up a picture of Eliot Ness spending his day trashing bootleg stills before coming home after work to pour himself a relaxing gin and tonic, an SRU committee man really *was* untouchable.

The Scots were never remotely threatened by anything like broken-time payment claims, or a potential split between clubs, given that their own game had not only begun in the public schools, but had kept its power-base there as well – both in the schools themselves, and in the Old Boys clubs known in Scotland as the Former Pupils. Even when Scottish rugby spread to the Borders – Hawick, Kelso, Gala, Langholm – it was as no more than a recreational respite from the hard toil of farming.

When the Scots jumped in to protest at the 1908/9 Australians' daily allowance of three shillings, it was to launch a climate of moral witch-hunting that was to last until the game went professional in 1995, and so indignantly did Scotland stand behind this inviolate principle that it probably denied them their most historic victory over the 1924/25 All Blacks – the Invincibles v the Untouchables, the match that never took place. The reasons for Scotland, who at that time possessed one of the finest teams in their history, declining to play the New Zealanders, had its origins in the 1905 All

Black visit. The SFU's attention was drawn, three years after the tour, to an RFU balance sheet listing an entry of expenditure which amounted to £1041, and when the Scots queried it, their English counterparts informed them that it concerned the three bob a day allowance for the tourists. This caused such apoplexy north of the border that they probably debated spending a similar amount on extra brickwork for Hadrian's Wall, but settled instead for cancelling – on moral grounds – the 1909 game against Australia. Paying expenses was nothing new . . . the RFU had agreed to pay travelling expenses to the home international teams in 1880.

This created its own row within the home unions, with the International Board voting that the Scots had no right to cancel any fixture without reference to them and further stating that the players who had received the daily cash allowance had not violated their amateur status. Nonetheless, this latter motion only just failed – the vote was 4–4 – and it lead to the IB placating the Scots with the announcement that it would not be permitted to happen again. 'The making of any allowances to players in cash,' said the Board, 'is in the opinion of this committee contrary to the principles of amateur Rugby Football and in future no such allowance will be made to any player.'

When it came to making sure that they gave away absolutely nothing that could be termed a reward, Scottish attitudes were not even softened by the Great War. In their self-important occupation of the moral high ground, several thousand dead soldiers were clearly no reason not to remind the New Zealanders that they had been extremely naughty with their expenses all those years ago and the SRU, with a pomposity that not even the RFU at their most windbaggish has ever been able to match, informed the 1924/25 All Blacks that they would not be granting them a fixture.

Another slightly more valid reason for declining to play them was the fact that the RFU had once again displayed the arrogant side of their nature by making the tour arrangements themselves, with a fine disregard for an agreement that it should be handled by the IB. However, far more pertinent was the fact that the Scots were still sulking over their own financial cock-up regarding the 1905 All Blacks. Dave Gallaher's side had asked for a guarantee of £200 for the international at Inverleith, which was the going rate, but some bright sparks on the SRU committee had concluded that the visitors were unlikely to be much of an attraction, and that two hundred quid represented a bit of a gamble. The best way, so the Scots thought, of insuring against being out of pocket, was to offer the All Blacks any profits (i.e., in their own minds, 0d.) from the match once they had claimed their own expenses for staging the game. It stuck in the craw, not to mention the memory, when the fans flocked in, and the SRU treasurer could barely keep his quill hand from trembling as he made out a cheque for £1700.

The fact that an unforgetting – not to mention unforgiving – nature is part of the Scottish psyche was graphically illustrated by a scarcely believable episode in 1920, involving the Gala forward Jock Wemyss. When Jock reported to the Scottish dressing room for the match against France in Paris, he found fourteen jerseys hanging neatly from their pegs, but nothing from his. 'Excuse me,' said Jock, to one of the RFU officials, 'but I don't appear to have a jersey.' 'Yes you have,' replied the alickadoo. 'We gave you one in 1914.' The fact that Jock only half blinked at this had something to do with having lost one of his eyes during the 1914–18 war, and he doubtless offered the pathetic excuse that his failure to remember where he'd put a jersey awarded six years earlier for his first cap against Wales was down to having one or two other things on his mind – such as shrapnel flying around his head.

Wemyss later got himself into further hot water for failing to cast his one remaining eye over the SRU small print regarding their own bye-law forbidding players from writing articles on the game in return for money. Jock had taken to writing the odd piece after officially retiring from rugby, but was then nailed when he agreed to a one-off appearance for Leicester in a mid-week holiday game against Heriot's at Inverleith six months later. If he didn't get shell-shock in the trenches, he'd certainly contracted a bad case of it in his postwar experiences with the Scottish Rugby Union.

A further example of just how far the SRU was prepared to go in protecting the amateur code came when it was revealed that the Newport players had received gold watches, worth £21 each, after their undefeated season in 1922–23. Neil McPherson, of Newport and Scotland, was invited to hand back his gift, and when McPherson told them where they could go, the SFU not only banned him *sine die*, but also placed a blanket ban on all Scottish clubs playing Newport. The case was brought before the IB, who ruled that all such mementoes should not have a greater value than £2. At that point the ban on McPherson was removed, although he was never capped again, doubtless because he was not playing well enough rather than for any vindictive reasons.

There was almost nothing, around this time, that did not cause the Scots to get a thistle up their kilts, and the SRU's next objection concerned numbering. Players in international trial matches wore numbered jerseys, but this was only to help selectors identify them, and the Scots considered it far too radical for mere spectators to be offered the same kind of assistance, and probably a bit vulgar, as well. Numbers were worn for the first time in an international championship match for Wales v England in 1922, and Ireland made the change in 1926. However, in Scotland it was not until 1928 that there was any challenge to the SRU's po-faced stance, when the RFU wrote requesting that the Scots wore numbers for that year's international against England. However, the Scottish RU committee charged with dealing with the issue had already considered themselves vindicated when their own players, upon being invited to make their preference known before the 1928 game against France, signed a letter declaring that they would rather go un-numbered.

> *You can't play first-class Rugger if you are dressed third-class, any more than you can sit on a public vehicle while a lady is standing, and remain a gentleman.*
>
> AN OLD BEDFORD BOY on 'Some Rudiments Of Rugger'

The RFU, whether through their own conviction that numbers were a desirable innovation or simply the age-old story of wanting to get up Scottish noses, decided to air the matter in the press, much to the chagrin of the Scots, whose own business was invariably conducted in such a way as eventually to be adopted as a role model for the Soviet Politburo. King George V even got involved, expressing his puzzlement over Scotland's reluctance, although nothing could have been more calculated to entrench their views than a note of dissent from the ruling English monarch. Jock Aikman Smith of the SRU apparently took exception to being lectured by Buckingham Palace, and said before the game against England: 'This is a rugby match, not a cattle auction.' During this period in rugby history, the only monarch on the same wavelength as the SRU was Canute, and it was to be another four years before the Scots finally relented over the numbering business.

No price was too high to pay for the Scots in their zealotry, and the decision not to play the 1924/25 Invincibles is still talked about today. In the mid-20s, Scotland arguably had the finest side in their history, and no sooner had the All Blacks returned to New Zealand than Scotland clinched their first Grand Slam in the brand new surroundings of Murrayfield. There was no victory over New Zealand to celebrate, though, neither has there ever been. After another failed expedition to New Zealand at the start of the new millennium, Scotland have never beaten the All Blacks, and they wonder still about what the outcome might have been had the 1924/25 match taken place.

Arguments with New Zealanders over expenses, however, were only a minor blip on the Scots' more regular agenda of locking horns with the auld enemy, England. At a very early stage in rugby's development, the RFU was identified by the Scots (not without justification) as being yet another symbol of 2000 years of English arrogance, and many of the early contests between the sides were as notable for generating ill-feeling as football matches between Rangers and Celtic. As far as the Scots were concerned, the self-appointed autocracy of the RFU was the sporting equivalent of being ordered about in their general lives by Westminster, and it is a constant source of surprise to many that the only man to have attempted blowing up the Houses of Parliament was caught wearing a pair of trousers rather than a kilt. Had it been Hamish McFawkes instead of plain old Guy, 5 November would be a national Scottish holiday.

Scotland won the first-ever international against England at Raeburn Place in 1871, but it was the draw in the 1881 match – the Scots equalising with a late goal – that prompted a mutual exchange of sneering, beginning with the RFU president's patronising post-match comment. 'The Scotch [sic] team was strong,' he said, before adding a withering PS to this apparent compliment. 'Their strength being in umpiring.'

Not to put too fine a point on it, the English were accusing the Scottish umpires of being bent, and the RFU president's demand to 'in future have unbiased referees who understand their duties' provoked a predictable avalanche of correspondence between the two Unions. This time, however, there was a positive outcome. The following year, England's invitation to an Irish referee to officiate in the game at Manchester was not only accepted by the Scots, but they also adopted the principle themselves for their own home games.

Furthermore, the Scots also made it clear to the RFU that there was nothing personal in their annual slanging matches by the fact that they also spent a lot of their time squabbling between themselves. When R.W. Irvine retired in 1881, after captaining the side for the previous five years, a row erupted over his successor, resulting in a failed attempt to overturn the committee. Peace eventually broke out, although several Scottish forwards – including A.G. Petrie, the senior man in the pack who had been passed over for the captaincy – withdrew from the team for the Irish match, with the result that it was lost for the first time. However, plenty of energy was always reserved for doing battle with the RFU, which, as we have seen previously, resulted in the Scots, Irish and Welsh all declining to play England for two seasons between 1888 and 1889.

Unlike the English, the Scots waged their verbal wars purely through passion, as opposed to anything Machiavellian, and the way they played their rugby was much the same. Their trademark, already established, was feet, feet and more feet. They were masters of the foot rush from the wheeling scrum, and opposing defenders taking the plucky option of falling on the ball in the face of Scottish marauding went down on it in the knowledge that they might shortly be requiring the services of a plastic surgeon, never mind a trainer.

The Scottish tactics were actually quite skilful, not least in that the balls of that era were much less pointed than they are today, and easier to dribble. One of the great Scottish forwards of the day was a doctor called MacMyn, and he would practise by dribbling a rugby ball while his dog chased around trying to get it off him. MacMyn also devised a method of kicking the ball forwards with backspin on it, so that it often bounced back towards his own team.

The Scots were the most adventurous of the home nations when it came to blooding youngsters, and when they won the Triple Crown in 1903, they chose – or attempted to – a fifteen-year-old schoolboy by the name of Kenneth Grant McLeod. However, young Kenneth's headmaster, Dr Head, decided that his maths lessons came first and refused him permission to play. McLeod had to wait another two seasons before being picked – along with his brother – against Gallaher's 1905 All Blacks.

The All Blacks were also the only international side more used to cold winters than the Scots, and the weather north of the border certainly had a hand in Scotland's famous 1906 victory over South Africa in front of 32,000 at Hampden Park. The Springbok forward W.A. Millar graphically recalled: 'every southerner in the vicinity was groping for his nose, and shivering like a dude on a dentist's doorstep.' The Springbok captain, when he'd thawed out, complimented the Scots on 'a wonderful pack of forwards'. This was another Triple Crown year for Scotland.

Scotland enjoyed some memorable moments in the 1920s, including, in 1923, their first win in Cardiff for thirty-three years. Their first try was scored by Eric Liddell, who was to break the 400 metres world record and take the gold medal at the 1924 Olympic Games in Paris the following year. Paris was the last time rugby was included as an Olympic sport, which goes some way towards explaining why the current Olympic champions are the USA.

It had become increasingly clear that Inverleith was too small to cope with increasing spectator interest for the big internationals, and the Scots were also keen to match the English, who had recently found an impressive new home at Twickenham. Although some western-based clubs were pressing the claims of Hampden Park, Edinburgh was always the favoured city, and it was J. Aikman Smith who reported the possibility of acquiring the nineteen acres of Murrayfield belonging to the Edinburgh Polo Club. Within three months, in 1922, it belonged to the SRU. The Scots quickly made it into a natural theatre for rugby, and Murrayfield's raised embankments were a famous sight for over fifty years.

In March 1925, the Scots found themselves going for the Grand Slam against an England side who had not been beaten for thirteen championship matches, and more than 70,000 spectators were crammed inside the new Murrayfield stadium to see a game in which the Scots trailed by 6 points with fifteen minutes remaining. Wallace's try and Gillies' conversion cut that to 1 point, and with the final minute approaching, fly half Herbert Waddell dropped the winning goal. After the 1925 Grand Slam, the Scots stuck it up the English again the following year, winning for the first time at Twickenham, and the following year made it three in a row over the auld enemy, 21–13, in front of a record Murrayfield crowd of 80,000. The 1920s era gave birth to many great players, among them the so-called Flying Scotsman, winger Ian Smith. Eric Liddell may have grabbed belated glory as one of the 'stars' of the Oscar-winning *Chariots of Fire* but Smith's story has no need of an inventive scriptwriter.

Smith, a sprinter, did not play rugby at school, nor at Oxford until he began dating a girl from Cambridge, and took up the game in an attempt – successful by all accounts – to get her to change her allegiance to dark blue. Within a year he had won his blue, and within two years he was playing for Scotland. In one game against Wales Smith scored four tries, and he got four more in the 1925 international against France. At the dinner afterwards, so Scottish rugby folklore has it, Smith sat next to a Frenchman who, despite obvious language difficulties (there are a lot of Scots who can't understand fellow Scots, never mind Frenchmen), attempted to engage him in conversation. Smith, thinking he had been asked how many tries he scored, replied modestly; 'Four or five, I think,' whereupon the Frenchman, in a flurry of astonished 'Mon dieu's, fell back into his chair. The question had actually been how many seconds it took him to run the 100 yards.

CHAPTER 8

BRAIN AND BRAWN

ENGLAND HAVE NEVER BEEN seriously challenged as the most unloved side in the northern hemisphere, and this somewhat dubious honour has only once been known to change hands south of the equator. However, New Zealand – ruthless, single-minded and hugely efficient – held on to it only for as long as the South Africans spent in sporting isolation. Once the men in green returned, it was not even a serious contest.

It is mostly down to national stereotyping. Off the field, the New Zealanders are regarded as quiet, warm-hearted, friendly people, whereas the white South African is looked upon as cold, unbending and arrogant. Apartheid is the reason, with rugby football in South Africa, from its very beginnings there, perceived as the ultimate symbol of white supremacy. Even after majority rule, and the apparently unifying appearance of Nelson Mandela in a green and gold Springbok jersey during the 1995 World Cup final, South Africa's rugby team remained an object of loathing for many who grew up among the country's disenfranchised majority, and when the British Lions won the Test series there in 1997, the dancing in the streets was not exclusively confined to the travelling supporters from Britain. When the Lions won the first Test in Cape Town, an article in a Cape Coloured magazine rejoiced in what it saw as a desperate blow to the Afrikaner psyche. 'They are so arrogant they don't even know themselves how unpopular they are. They hate the blacks, they don't like the Brits, and, come to that, they don't much care for each other.'

However, there is also another way to become deeply unpopular outside your own supporters, and that is to win a lot. The Springboks have never enjoyed the near mythical status of the All Blacks, but South Africa have generally been more consistent and tougher to beat. In fact, in the century-old duel between these two rugby titans, it has been the men in green who have held the upper hand for longer, culmi-nating in their surprise victory over the 1995 World Cup hot favourites New Zealand. What is not in doubt is that New Zealand and South Africa, and more latterly Australia, have ruled rugby's roost for almost as long as the game itself.

British colonisation of Southern Africa is almost certainly what gave rugby its early foothold there, although the game was ultimately annexed - and given the national identity it still holds today - by the Dutch Afrikaner. The oldest club, Hamilton in Cape Town, was founded in 1875, although it did not switch to the Rugby School code until three years later. The original game there had been based on the Winchester School code, brought to South Africa by Canon G. Ogilvie. Everyone knew him as Gog, as that was all that could be deciphered from his signature.

Rugby suited the environment and the lifestyle perfectly. The Boer War was an often brutal and unchivalrous conflict, which spawned gratuitous acts of cruelty and, long before the Third Reich, concentration camps. And yet, in 1902, hostili-ties were brought to a temporary halt for a game of rugby between the opposing forces – just as the butchery in the Great War was put on hold while the Germans and the Allies linked up for a game of soccer on Christmas Day. The Germans probably won that on penalties as well. The permit for that temporary truce in South Africa is now in the South African Rugby Board museum. It was a letter from General S.G. Maritz of the Transvaal Scouting Corps addressed to the British commander, Major Edwards. Edwards had mooted the idea to the opposition forces, and Maritz replied: 'Dear Sir, I wish to inform you that I have agreed to a rugby match taking place between you and us. I, from my side, will agree to a cease-fire tomorrow from 12 o'clock until sunset, the time and venue of the match to be arranged by you in consultation with Messrs Roberts and Van Rooyen who I am sending to you.'

The British – in the form of the first-ever Lions – had toured South Africa eleven years earlier in 1891 under the captaincy of W.E. (Bill) Maclagan, with financial guarantees for the trip underwritten by Cecil Rhodes, who was at that time Prime Minister of the Cape Colony. Rhodes had sailed to South Africa on the *Dunottar Castle* with a gold cup presented by Donald Currie of the Castle Shipping Line, to be presented to the South African side that put up the best opposition (no one was expected to win) against the British. It was won by Griqualand West, who lost by a try to nil. They in turn presented the Cup to the SARB. Eventually, the Currie Cup – as it did in cricket – became the title of South Africa's inter-provincial competition.

There were three Tests played between South Africa and the tourists, the Lions winning 4–0, 3–0 and 4–0 – a bit of a Bore War, it would seem. Two members of the Lions party, incidentally, Dr Tommy Crean and Robert Johnson, were to return in somewhat more hostile circumstances, both winning Victoria Crosses in the war against the Boers.

Before that, the Lions returned in 1896 to discover tougher opposition and, although the series was won, the Lions were beaten in the final Test against a side captained by Barrie

Heatlie and wearing for the first time the famous green jerseys. Further proof of rugby's grip on white South Africa came in 1903, when, despite the Boer War being such a recent memory that they had barely got around to burying all the dead, the Lions were invited back again. This time South Africa won – and were not to lose another Test series for more than half a century.

The famous South African green was not officially adopted until their first tour of Britain in 1906/07. They were immediately invited after the success of the 1905 All Blacks. If it hadn't been for an impromptu meeting of the tour management, they might have inherited the slightly less intimidating nickname of the Scruffs as opposed to the Springboks. The tour manager was J.C. Carden, who wrote afterwards: 'No uniforms or blazers had been provided for us, and we were a motley turnout at practice at Richmond. That evening I spoke to [tour officials] Roos and Carolin and pointed out that the witty London press would invent some funny name for us if we didn't invent one ourselves. We thereupon agreed to call ourselves the Springboks, and to tell the pressmen that we desired to be so named.'

Carden went on: 'The reason I remember this so distinctly is that Paul [Roos] reminded us that the correct plural in Afrikaans for a Springbok was "Springbokken". However, the *Daily Mail*, after our first practice, called us Springboks and the name stuck. I at once ordered the dark green gold-edged blazers, and still have the first Springbok badge that was ever made.'

It was a tour that made famous names of the Stellenbosch threequarters, or the 'Thin Red Line' as Bob Loubser, Japie Krige, Anton Stegmann and Boy de Villiers were collectively known. The Springboks had a habit in those days of using names like 'Boy' for players who were young, and yet were physically more intimidating than most of their elders. The New Zealanders were a bit like that also and, had Jonah Lomu been playing in the early 1900s, he would almost certainly

have been known as Tiny. Krige was known as the Artful
Dodger, while Loubser, twenty-two, could run the 100 yards
in ten seconds. He was unusual in that he invariably carried
the ball in one hand, the left, while running at the opposition,
claiming that using both slowed him up. Loubser missed only
six of the twenty-eight games and scored twenty-four tries.
The Springbok backs were fast and direct, just as they are
today, while the forwards, as now, were noted for their sheer
physical presence. Most of them were manual labourers,
working for most of the day under a hot sun, and they fed
themselves, almost literally, on raw meat. Even today, you
won't find too many vegetables on the menu at a South
African braai.

The South Africans won all their first fifteen matches on
tour, only to come unstuck – or perhaps more accurately,
stuck – in the mud of Hampden Park against the Scots. It
was a foul, wet afternoon, perfect for the marauding foot
rushes of the home forwards and, unlike the All Blacks, the
Springboks have more often than you might expect found
Scotland to be difficult opponents.

A colour clash with the Irish forced them to change shirts
for the next international (needless to say, they chose white)
and while they won that one narrowly, many expected them
to lose to the conquerors of the All Blacks, Wales. A record
crowd of 45,000 turned up at St Helen's, and tensions were
high on both sides when the Welsh captain Gwyn Nicholls
entered the Springbok dressing room before the kick-off and
threw a ball towards Paul Roos for him to check over.

'I suppose we may as well toss,' said Nicholls, whereupon
Roos tossed the ball back to him and said, 'How do you
propose to toss with this?' It may have been one of the first
recorded attempts of humour from an Afrikaner, in which
case it is pretty clear why it happens rather infrequently. More
likely, it was an indication of how fired-up the tourists were
to succeed where the All Blacks had failed, and the Springboks
produced their best performance of the tour to win 11–0.

The match against England was the one in which Dr A. Alcock of Guy's Hospital is alleged to have won his only cap as the result of a clerical cock-up involving an invitation that should have gone to L.A.N. Slocock, although the good doctor couldn't have been a complete waste of space as the home team held the tourists to a 3–3 draw. It was another player winning his only cap, Freddie Brooks, who scored England's equalising try, from a miskick that went straight to him. It wasn't a very neighbourly act from a winger who played for Rhodesia – Brooks was only playing because he happened to be on holiday in England at the time. South Africa's worst result of the tour was in their final match against Cardiff on New Year's Day. Mentally, they probably had one foot on the boat taking them back home to the sunshine, and in ankle-deep mud and a howling crosswind, they went down 17–0.

Conditions had been pretty similar throughout the tour, and the Springboks' hard running style was much easier to reproduce when they were back on their own sunbaked turf for the visit of the 1910 Lions. They won the series 2–1, and were back in Britain – the shorter sea passage made playing contacts much easier than with New Zealand and Australia – in the winter of 1912/13.

Their captain, Billy Millar, had actually been the last name down on the selectors' list when they picked the side, but when their original choice of captain was vetoed by the executive board – for reasons they kept to themselves – they met again, chose Millar, and this time had the appointment approved. This scenario was repeated on the Springboks' short tour to Ireland and Scotland in 1965, when the selectors' original choice of Doug Hopwood was turned out by the executive board, who appointed Avril Malan instead.

Millar had been an invalid in his youth, and took up road walking in order to rebuild his health and strength. He became so proficient at the sport that he won a South African walking title, as well as becoming heavyweight boxing champion of the Cape Colony. A permanently damaged left arm was a comparatively small price to pay for surviving the 1914–18 war, but it ended Millar's rugby career, and he went into administration. Six Springboks failed to return from the war, with South Africa's loyalties to the old country prompting so many young men to join up that at Newlands a Roll of Honour to those who fell from the Western Province RU runs to a list of 272 names.

Before he volunteered for service, however, Millar had led his tour party to the Grand Slam – victory over all four home nations – which not even the All Blacks managed to achieve until 1978. Millar's squad had a pack to match its hard running backs, and began the long-standing tradition of South African touring teams presenting a Springbok head to the first side to beat them. On this occasion – they lost three times outside the Tests – the honour went to Newport at Rodney Parade.

Scotland were the first of the home nations to go under, beaten 16–0, and a week later the Springboks inflicted what was then a Test record defeat of 38–0 on the Irish. The Welsh match, a fortnight later, was played in the traditional wind and mud (quite how Manchester receives the accolade of rain capital of Britain ahead of Cardiff is something of a mystery) and Millar was a worried man when his side turned round only 3–0 ahead, having had the wind at their backs. However, they defended so stoutly that Wales's only real chance was restricted to a penalty, which was blown inches wide on the wind.

Finally they moved on to Twickenham, where England's unbeaten record fell, despite an early try from Ronnie Poulton. Victory over the English was the sweetest prize of all up until that point, but that was to change forever for the Springboks when an invitation to tour New Zealand in 1921 launched the biggest ongoing rivalry in international rugby – the Boks versus the Blacks, part rugby, part war, and not for the squeamish.

The All Blacks were heavy favourites to win on their own turf, but were surprised by the strength of the Springbok forwards, including Frank Mellish, a veteran of the Somme and Ypres, who had previously played for England. Mellish went on to serve in the Second World War, with the SA Armoured Division in North Africa, and rose to the rank of Colonel. The pre-tour forecasts looked pretty accurate when New Zealand took the first Test, which included a remarkable eighty-five-yard try by the All Blacks' Jack Steel. What made it remarkable was the fact that, having taken an awkward pass inside his own 25, Steel covered the next sixty yards juggling with the ball behind his back in a desperate attempt to regain control of it. It presumably had the effect of mesmerising the visitors as well, as Steel had only a few yards left to go when he finally got both hands on the ball – 'the try of the century' as it was described by one New Zealand newspaper.

Injuries forced the Springboks to make several changes for the second Test, including the selection in the centre of their lightest ever player, Billy Sendin, who at 8st 3lbs was better qualified to be a jockey. Despite being under strength, however, the Boks won the match and squared the series when Gerhard Morkel dropped a goal from the halfway line, and celebrated with a drink when a spectator on the popular side offered him a bottle. In a soccer match of such intensity, he would probably have had it thrown at him – not that the crowds were anything other than passionate. South Africa had visited Australia on an earlier part of the tour, and Morkel – having flattened a local hero with a tackle that flirted with the border-lines of legality – had to be smuggled out of the ground to escape the attentions of an angry crowd. Morkel faced a different off-pitch problem in New Zealand a week before the final Test. When he turned up at the seaside ground where he had been practising, he discovered that the goalposts were no longer there. The groundsman informed him that the locals had hidden them in the hope that he would lose his kicking form. It worked up to a point. Morkel hit an upright with a kick that would have won South Africa the series in a final

Above: A.L. Stoddart, lining up a pass for Blackheath in the 1890s – either that, or testing the ripeness of a honeydew melon outside the greengrocers.

Left: Is it a ruck? Is it a maul? An eighteenth-century mêlée at Rugby School – presumably before the 'use it or lose it' rule.

Below: Ireland defeat England in Dublin, 1900. In the days, by the looks of it, when the players outnumbered the spectators.

Inquisitive Old Gentleman, "WHO'S WON?"
First Football Player, "WE'VE LOST!"
Inquisitive Old Gentleman, "WHAT HAVE YOU GOT IN THAT BAG?"
Second Football Player, "THE UMPIRE"

Taking home the Christmas turkey – the turkey being the ref.

Wandsworth Prison Select XV? Guy's Hospital, with surgical caps at the ready? No it's the Cambridge XV, 1877.

'These shorts are a bit on the tight side.' W.W. Wakefield, 1927.

'Can't miss with these lightweight Nike boots.' George Nepia taking a kick at goal, 1924.

'I could just as easily have called a cab, but thanks for the lift anyway, boys.' Scottish rugby international Eric Liddell, paraded around Edinburgh University after winning the 400 metres at the 1924 Paris Olympics.

London Society of Rugby Referees Course of Instruction, 1949. 'Observe closely. This is what happens when two Scottish captains toss the coin.' 'It's mine!' 'No, it's mine.'

Members of the 1964 Fijian touring team, shortly before busking was prohibited on Paddington Station.

olin Meads, the New Zealand lock, ught up with Catchpole in a confined ace, and that was that.

Ken Catchpole, the Australian scrum half, gets the ball away before Meads arrives.

iff Morgan, Lions v SA, Johannesburg,)55. A Springbok flanker adopts an d rugby maxim. If you can't stop the 'elsh playing, a sharp blow to the indpipe might at least stop them iging.

Tony O'Reilly runs out for Ireland, 1956, in the days when he took the team bus to the ground with the rest of the lads instead of arriving by chauffeured limo.

Gareth Edwards gets the ball away in Sydney, 1969, just before cleaning up the cameraman.

Barry John, 'The King'. In the religion of Welsh rugby, John's No.10 jersey was holier than the Shroud of Turin.

Don Clarke's right boot is, for once, out of the picture as he arrives too late to stop Bev Risman scoring for the Lions against New Zealand, Auckland, 1959.

atty? Or just a bit cantankerous? New ealand's Grant Batty has a slight ifference of opinion with Barbarian om David.

Willie Duggan being introduced to South Africa's 'Dr Rugby', Danie Craven. 'It's an honour to meet you Dr Craven.' 'Yes, I know.'

he All Blacks' Bill Bush spots Graham rice out of position, and decides to urn a tight head into a loose one.

Welsh flanker Paul Ringer, sent off in the infamous 1980 international at Twickenham, is a sensitive soul, and finds the rest of it far too nasty to watch.

'This'll confuse 'em – if it doesn't confuse us first.' Spot the Ball Competition, New South Wales v England, 1975.

'Blimey, sarge. I'm not sure this helmet is big enough.' 'Don't worry, lad, they'll never hold up in court.'

Test billed, in that understated way they have in the southern hemisphere, as 'The Battle for World Supremacy'. The match finished 0–0, the series was drawn, and with the entire rugby world keenly awaiting the re-match, the 1928 series established the All Blacks v the Springboks as the ultimate confrontation.

New Zealand had by then advanced their reputation still further following the 1924–25 Invincibles tour of the British Isles, and nine of those players survived for the trip to South

Africa three years later. This time it was a four-Test series and, once again, it ended in a draw. South Africa won the first Test easily 17–0, New Zealand took the second 7–6, South Africa the third 11–6, and New Zealand the fourth (the so-called 'Umbrella Test' played in the kind of downpour rarely seen outside a tropical rainforest) 13–5.

The All Blacks might have won had they not still been sticking rigidly to their seven-man scrummage, and they were driven downfield time and again by the line-kicking of the Springbok fly half Bennie Osler. Mark Nicholls, one of the visiting players, said: 'No one knows better than a tired forward or a harassed back the feeling of security and relief which a long and accurate touch finder can give to his side. After each kicking duel, we invariably found that he had lost 30 to 40 yards.'

While the All Blacks had been the innovators at the start of the century, it was now the turn of their southern hemisphere rivals. The Springboks had already produced great physical players, but now they went a step further with great tactical players. It was Osler, in the late 1920s, who became the first truly great game-controlling fly half, and in the 1930s it was scrum half Danie Craven who introduced any number of new variations, including the dive-pass.

Benjamin Louwrens Osler, who played seventeen consecutive Tests for the Springboks, was revered in his own country, which gives you some idea of the South African ethos of not caring how ugly a game might be as long as their own team wins. Not to put too fine a point on it, Osler was a one-dimensional bore, who more or less turned the tactical clock all the way back to Rugby School by booting the ball at every available opportunity. Osler's kicking game earned him the nickname of Evil Genius, and one newspaper critic wrote of him: 'He evolved a fly-half game all his own, and his three-quarters had to subordinate their individual merits and ability to the type of game he favoured in a particular match.' Up until then, rugby had developed into a fifteen-man game, with the All Blacks demonstrating the value of keeping the ball in hand, even in tight defensive situations. To play outside Osler, however, was to run the risk – like all the other spectators – of being charged admission money. Another South African fly half who achieved adulatory status in his own country was Naas Botha, and if Botha's inside centre ever received a pass, he had to be revived with smelling salts.

Danie Craven, who played in seven internationals with Osler, remembers one particular match in which the crowd had begun to get more than a tad irritated at the number of Osler-induced line-outs, and after yet another thumping boot straight into touch, a chorus of booing started up. 'Give me ball again, Danie, and I won't disappoint them,' said Osler. Thump. Straight back into touch. More booing. Thump. Another one straight out, and this time less booing. Eventually the crowd, who realised that they were having no effect at all on Osler, stopped booing, at which point the fly half turned to Craven and said, 'That's better. They are beginning to mind their manners.'

The Springboks toured Britain in 1931/32, travelling this time on the *Windsor Castle*. The perils of practising in those days cost them the services of Jock van Niekerk. He damaged his knee so badly trying to stop one of three lost balls on the voyage to the UK that his tour and career was over. Again the Springboks completed the Grand Slam, losing only to the Midland Counties at Leicester, but their ten-man style was heavily criticised. Osler admitted: 'I played the worst rugby of my career on that tour. It's true that our backline as a whole did not come up to expectation, but I was the big culprit. Friends have tried to cover for me, but the truth is that I was right off form.'

His young scrum half, Craven, went on to make his mark as South Africa's 'Dr Rugby' for the next forty years, as player, coach and administrator. He and Osler were as cerebral a pair of half backs as the game has seen, and one of Osler's tactical triumphs on that tour was the curious instruction to his forwards not to, on any account, win any line-out ball. It came at half-time in the Wales match, with the home team leading 3–0, and Osler and his backline creating nothing. 'Let them have the ball,' said Osler, 'and we'll play on their handling errors.' And it worked.

South Africa's steady rise to the top was further accentuated by New Zealand travelling backwards in the 1930s, and on their 1935/36 tour of Britain, the All Blacks lost to Wales, Swansea and England. Wales by this time had unearthed Haydn Tanner who, as a schoolboy, had not only played in the Swansea victory, but was taken to the international game by his gym mistress as he had never been to Cardiff on his own before. The match at Twickenham, won by England 13–0, came to be remembered for the classic individual try from Prince Obolensky, the Russian aristocrat killed in a flying accident in the Second World War who would certainly be embroiled in birth certificate investigations if he had been playing today.

A couple of years later Phil Nel's Springboks at last broke the deadlock against New Zealand by beating them 2–1, despite losing the opening Test in Wellington after dropping the skipper, playing Craven at fly half and being without the injured Boy Louw and Gerry Brand. All came back for the rest of the series, and Craven moved back to scrum half, to inflict the first-ever home series defeat suffered by the All Blacks. South Africa were crowned the unofficial world champions. South Africa's squad included a forward with the unusual name of Ebbo Bastard, which, given the peculiarities of the southern hemisphere vowel, sounds as though he might have been an ethnic Aboriginal of dubious parentage. However, it really was his real name.

South Africa managed to beat New Zealand, despite some nasty experiences on the first leg of the tour in Australia. There, the Australians attempted to do their neighbours a rare favour by turning the Springboks' boat across the Tasman

Sea into a hospital ship. South Africa won both Tests there, but the second – which left scrum half Pierre de Villiers unconscious, and several team-mates minus a few teeth – was comfortably the dirtiest international ever played until that point. South Africa led 26–0 at the break, but Australia decided to make a fight of it in the second half. When Pierre de Villiers was stretchered off unconscious, Aussie Aub Hodgson and Harry Martin belted hell out of each other in a stand-up fight. Hodgson had driven straight at de Villiers and handed him the ball. This was the signal for Hodgson and the rest of the Aussie forwards to steamroller all over the scrum half.

However, it was the potential bruising to national pride which drove South Africa on to recover from possible disaster in New Zealand. After losing the opening Test, the Springboks trailed 6–0 in the second international, but got it back to within a point before Gerry Brand squeezed them home with a 55-yard penalty. They were helped by a badly concussed Boy Louw, who couldn't stop giggling after his bang on the head, which both sets of forwards found disconcerting – although it didn't put off the All Black prop Dalton who kept coming through the line-out and clobbering Craven, whether he had the ball or not. Craven called on Louw for help, indicating that he should block the gap in the line-out. Louw must have misunderstood because at the next line-out he piled into Dalton with everything and the prop was left lying in a heap. Craven was rather embarrassed, especially when Louw inquired if that was what he wanted.

'No, but it will do,' responded the Springbok scrum half.

After two previously deadlocked series, here they were again at 1–1 with a game to go. Before this deciding match, the All Blacks had been steadily coming to terms with South Africa's greater firepower at the line-out, and were confident of more than matching them this time. However, the Springboks had been working massively hard on their scrum-mage, and when they were awarded a line-out in the New

Zealand 25 in the opening minutes, they opted for a scrum instead. The Springboks scored from it, and were never threatened in the entire match.

The following year the British Lions lost again in South Africa, and the only thing that managed to put a temporary halt to the Springboks' continuing domination of world rugby was a rather more serious skirmish known as the Second World War.

CHAPTER 9

IRELAND EXPECTS: THE PHANTOM PREGNANCY

W E'RE ALL FAMILIAR WITH the old Irish joke about the tourist who stops to ask directions in Connemara, or some such place, and is told, 'if I were you, I wouldn't start from here.' Well, much the same applies to Irish rugby, which started from the wrong place and has continued to enchant us with its chaotic sense of direction ever since. Fergus Slattery was the most eloquent of men, but even he might have been left speechless when he was involved in one of those situations that could only happen to the Irish. When Ireland arrived in Fiji to play an unofficial international on their way home from a tour to Australia, they discovered that the opposition were actually playing someone else in another part of the world. The Irish Rugby Union later admitted that they had failed to confirm the fixture, and ended up playing Fiji's B team.

Ireland are rugby's great under-achievers, who every now and then produce the kind of mini-surge that sparks off talk of a rebirth. However, the fact that Dublin's family planning clinics issue more morning-after pills during international match weekends than at any other time of the year (thus averting an outbreak of Angus O'Flahertys and Jean-Pierre Murphys in the telephone directory) seems even more apposite when the Irish rebirth invariably turns out to be nothing more than the latest in a long line of phantom pregnancies.

In international rugby the Irish have no serious rivals in the bon-viveur stakes, and are by some margin the best losers. When England won a match in Dublin 8–6 in the 1980s with two breakaway tries after Ireland had laid siege to their line for roughly seventy-eight of the eighty minutes, their captain Fergus Slattery said in the post-match interview that England had thoroughly deserved to win. It is the eye-patch syndrome in reverse. If the South Africans and the New Zealanders are classic examples of teams for whom winning is everything, then Ireland represent everything that the amateur game was originally meant to be. You could wander into any city centre pub or bar after a major international, and only in Dublin would you still not have a clue whether the home team had won or lost.

With England and Scotland having constantly updated and modernised their grounds, and Wales the proud tenants of the new Millennium Stadium in Cardiff, Ireland took their leave of the twentieth century still stuck in a kind of timewarp at the evocatively charming, yet dilapidated and outdated Lansdowne Road, albeit with plans to improve their arena. Even the introduction of painted logos on the field, seamlessly adopted by others, caused chaos in Ireland. The first time they were used at Lansdowne Road, the colours all ran in Dublin's afternoon rain and the players, especially hooker Keith Wood, wandered around looking as though they'd been caught in an explosion in a paint factory.

To understand the nature of Irish rugby, you have to go right back to the beginning, and their introduction to the international arena at the Kennington Oval in 1875. The famous Irish observer Jacques J. McCarthy noted that his team were 'immaculately innocent of training', the team turned up two men short, and the overall impression of chaos and disorganisation has remained with them ever since.

Yet, while England effortlessly split their own country in the way they administered the game, Ireland, for most of the past century a country scarred by a grievous political schism, has somehow managed to promote a consistently united front on the rugby field, even in the most hostile of times. Initially, the formation of the Irish Football Union in Dublin in 1874 did cause a bit of rift and, in a mild fit of pique across the border, the Northern Union was formed in Belfast. However, while Ireland was politically headed for an intransigent stand-off, the spirit of unity was swiftly applied in the rugby arena and north and south managed to bury their differences in the space of only five years. It has been that way, miraculously some would say, ever since.

Ireland's first match on home soil was at the Leinster Cricket Club in Dublin against England in 1876. Scotland were entertained in Belfast in 1877, and Lansdowne Road was used for the first time in 1878 for another visit from England. Only two men from the south played in the Belfast game, and it was clear to the Irish that they had to get their act – and their team – together. The last meeting of the IFU took place at 63 Grafton Street on 28 October, 1879 and the first meeting of the newly unified Irish Rugby Football Union took place at the same venue on 5 February the following year. There was a lot of optimism (isn't there always?) about things now taking a turn for the better – a none too difficult task given that Ireland's international record to that date was played 7, lost 7, points 0. Thomas Gordon won three caps in the 1870s for Ireland at half back and remains to this day, rugby's only one-handed international. He lost his hand in an accident at an early age.

Unification clearly had some kind of impact. Ireland at least managed to get on the scoreboard that year courtesy of a try by Trinity student John Loftus Cuppaidge against England at Lansdowne Road. They still lost, as they also did to Scotland. However, on 19 February, 1881 at Ormeau, just over a year after unification, they won at last when John Bagot's dropped goal was enough to beat Scotland's try.

The first match against Wales took place in January, 1882, although whether it could be described as the first-ever game of rugby between the sides is a moot point as it was mostly an exercise in determining who could inflict the most injuries. Two of the Irish players actually walked off the field in protest at the violence and, not surprisingly in the circumstances, Wales won by two goals and two tries to nil. Ten of the original Irish selection had withdrawn and the correspondent of the *Irish Times* referred to the 'dormant apathy' of the Irish team. Enough bad feeling remained for the 1883 fixture to be cancelled, but hostilities, so to speak, resumed in 1884, the first year of the full championship, when Ireland again demonstrated their ability for either starting or finishing a game with only thirteen men. As in their first-ever international, Ireland, finding trouble in raising a representative team to travel to Cardiff, turned up two men short and, despite pressing the IRFU secretary H.G. Cook into emergency service, they still had to borrow a couple of players from Newport. One of them, H.M. Jordan, later went on to play for Wales, although the other, H. McDaniel, had to content himself with winning his one and only cap for someone else's country.

If things were a little muddled on the field, it was only a reflection of the administrative side of things, and at the IRFU's annual meeting in 1883 the statement of accounts was rejected on the grounds of being 'quite unintelligible'. An investigation revealed that the Imperial Hotel in Belfast was still chasing payment for the 1881 Scotland dinner, and the players themselves (fifteen of them this time) were being pursued for a guinea each as their contribution for the meal. It wasn't as if it was a case of one department not knowing what the other was doing, either. That season's captain, George Scriven, for example, had an intimate knowledge of the affairs of both the chairman of selectors and the IRFU president, given that all three jobs were done by himself.

There was clearly no end to Scriven's talents. The following season he refereed the England–Scotland match, without much distinction, it would appear. There was a heated dispute over England's winning try, resulting in a cancellation of the 1885 fixture and the start of the process that led to the formation of the International Board.

Even in those days, the Irish did not feel inclined to scale down their post-match revelry by anything as inconsequential as losing, but in 1887 the celebrations rose above even Dublin's legendary standards when they beat the English for the first time at Lansdowne Road. It was more memorable for some Irish players than others, not least John Macaulay, who had used up all his annual leave at work and was about to withdraw from the team when he checked his conditions of employment and discovered that a ceremony of marriage brought with it the entitlement of an extra weekend off. Whether or not he shared this information with his prospective bride as he went down on one knee is not known, but get married he did – on the morning of the game. 'Now then, dear,' he doubtless said, as he led his new bride into some raucous Irish tavern after the game, 'about our wedding night . . .' Another peculiarity of that game concerned the Irish full back D.B. Walkington, who was so short-sighted that he took the field wearing a monocle.

Despite this win, Ireland continued to make a generally poor fist of things on the field, and for the first three years of the 1890s, they won just one of their twelve matches. Selection, as ever, was a pretty haphazard affair. In fact, the words 'selection committee' are not mentioned in any Union minutes until 1892, and the first record of an actual selection meeting does not appear until the 1894 AGM minutes.

Scotland, England and Wales had taken it in turns to win the first three Triple Crowns of that decade, but no one, least of all themselves, seriously thought that the Irish would complete the sequence in 1894. However, they began by winning in England for the first time, overcame Scotland by a single try, and then clung on to beat Wales in Belfast after a close-range penalty goal in the opening minutes. Typically, with the majority of that side still with them the following season, Ireland managed to lose every game – a familiar scenario for Irish supporters.

Just as typically, Ireland won the championship the following year, although a 0–0 draw with Scotland denied them the Triple Crown. Then, after beating England and Scotland in 1899, they headed for Cardiff in search of their second Triple Crown. The crowd was packed in so tightly that the enclosure rails kept giving way, and the play was held up time and again for the Cardiff police to clear the pitch. The Welsh full back, Billy Bancroft, disappeared into this crowd after one crunching tackle never to return. It must have been during one of those rare moments when the spectators were actually behind the touchline that the Irish wing G.P. Doran dived over in the corner for the winning try.

And so the nineteenth century ended with Irish rugby in sound heart, and looking forward in anticipation of more success in the twentieth. They didn't have to wait too long. Ireland duly collected Triple Crown number three after the death of three British monarchs, as well as the abdication of Edward VIII, the Russian Revolution, talking pictures, and two World Wars.

All through that forty-nine-year drought Ireland produced plenty of decent players, but not many good teams. Full back Ernie Crawford won thirty caps after making a late debut at the age of twenty-eight, and centre George Stephenson was a devastating tackler and runner. There was the traditional quota of characters, too, among them Jamie Clinch, a player who incited opposition crowds wherever he went with a style of play that owed little to subtlety. 'Send the dirty bastard off, ref!' came a cry from the crowd at a Wales–Ireland match in Swansea, not an unusual exhortation when Clinch was playing, but on this occasion it happened as Clinch ran on to the field before the kick-off.

Clinch once made a rare appearance in the centre for a charity match, and his love of physical contact led him to make not a single pass to his winger, the legendary Flying Scotsman, Ian Smith. After the game, the victorious opposition captain made a speech thanking Clinch for ignoring one of the finest wingers ever seen on a rugby field. Clinch got up and replied that, while Smith might have been the Flying Scotsman, he had a reputation to uphold as the Irish Mail. 'And as everyone knows,' said Clinch, 'the Irish mail is only slightly faster than the Irish female.'

Ireland had their moments in the 1920s. Wales denied them a Grand Slam in 1926, they shared the title in 1927, and won at Twickenham for the first time in 1929. However, some great individuals failed to gel as a team, and the 1930s were not much better either, despite Ireland claiming the championship in 1935. Just before the Second World War, Wales again denied them them a Triple Crown in their final match, fixtures in those days being played in the same order, as opposed to on a rotational basis.

By the end of the war, Irish optimism centred once again on a handful of talented individuals and their collective heart. The teamwork, support and organisation of sides such as the All Blacks and the Springboks were entirely foreign to the Irish nature. They much preferred to turn up on the day and see what happened – and it was this that bothered the opposition most. If the Irish themselves hadn't a clue what plan they had for that afternoon, then no one else did either. Plus, there was the Irish style of play to contend with. At Lansdowne Road in particular, Ireland were known as a 'kitchen sink' sort of side, and if the weather turned it into a physical, up-and-at-'em type of contest, it was no place for the faint-hearted.

Talented individuals were nothing new, which is probably why the Irish were not especially excited by a nineteen-year-old fly half by the name of Jackie Kyle, who made his debut in the unofficial international of 1946 against England. The programme notes read: 'a particularly straight, strong runner, he looks to have a great future.' In fact, thanks to Kyle, so did Ireland. The Irish used twenty-six players in that first postwar year of unofficial matches, but only two were to leave a lasting impression, both of them medical students – one from the south, hooker Karl Mullen of the Old Belvedere club, and one from the north, Kyle, from Queen's University.

Unusually, the Irish selectors declined to panic when the first official postwar international resulted in defeat at home to France, and in their next game Ireland thrashed England 22–0. It was the last cap won by full back Con Murphy, the only Irishman to be capped either side of the Second World War. Victory at Murrayfield set up yet another Triple Crown visit to Wales, but the omens were there when the game was postponed for three weeks because of frost, and began thirty-five minutes late when the Irish team were held up in traffic. Sure enough, the Welsh foiled them again.

There was no optimism at all when Ireland began the 1948 campaign in Paris with much the same side that had gone down to the touring Australians, but, as any follower of Irish rugby knows, there is no side quite like them for turning it on when it is least expected. It was just the one change in the side for Paris that was the catalyst that season – the introduction of Jim McCarthy to join Bill McKay and Des O'Brien in the back row. The Irish back-row tackling, especially from McKay, had always been fearsome, but McCarthy's running and support play was something new, dangerously close to teamwork, in fact. This unit now gave more space for Kyle to work his sorcery, and with a playmaker like Kyle in the side, Ireland, for just about the first time in their history, came perilously close to being controlled and organised. The opposition had always been worried by Irish harrying and marauding, but when they realised there was something going on in the cranial department as well, it was enough to induce panic. England were seen off by three tries to nil, and a Kyle try inspired them to victory over the Scots. The championship was secure, and now for the Triple Crown. As any Irishman at the time might have put it, bloody Wales again.

The thirteenth of March, 1948 is for many, the greatest day in Ireland's rugby history. They could have sold ten times the 30,000 tickets that represented Ravenhill's capacity, and the usually lethal combination of Wales and the Grand Slam meant that all over Ireland publicans were being asked for double brandy chasers along with the Guinness in an effort to calm the nerves. Karl Mullen, the captain, recalled: 'We were tense and anxious. Too much ball for the Welsh would probably spell disaster, and we feared Haydn Tanner, Bleddyn Williams and Ken Jones.'

However, when Ireland turned around level at 3–3, Mullen called what he described as a 'council of war', and Wales were constantly battered back towards their own line by the green hordes. 'When J.C. Daly got the [winning] try,' said Mullen, 'we played like men possessed.' Not quite as possessed as the crowd, however. The final whistle produced a mad stampede, and Chris Daly, playing what turned out to be his final game before turning professional, had the shirt ripped from his back.

Ireland started as warm favourites when they opened their 1949 campaign against France in Dublin and, as expected by now in such circumstances, lost. The defeat would have been even heavier had the International Board not by then reduced the value of the dropped goal from four points to three. However, wins over England and Scotland – the latter game marking the debut of centre Noel Henderson – sent Ireland once again over to Wales in search of the Triple Crown. The game was deadlocked until Kyle, breaking down the blind side, hoisted a high ball towards the Welsh line, which ended with McCarthy outjumping the home defence to score. Most people in the ground, with the important exception of English referee Tom Pearce, thought that McCarthy had arrived from an offside position, but it all added up to back-to-back Triple Crowns, for only the fourth time in home nations' history.

McCarthy, like Daly before him, had no jersey to keep or swap for a souvenir, as the Irish fans rushed on and tore it off his back.

The following year qualification became a big issue for the first time, when England fielded a team that included a couple of South Africans and a New Zealander. The result was an IB edict at the end of the season stating that no overseas player could be capped for anyone else after playing for his own country, although this was not something that concerned the Irish. Their own regulation, albeit unwritten, was to select players born in Ireland, or with at least one Irish parent, who had never so much as appeared in a trial game for another country.

Ireland's golden era was marked by the award of the Lions' captaincy to Karl Mullen that summer in a party containing nine Irishmen in all, including Kyle, Henderson and McCarthy. In 1951 Ireland won their third title in four years. Their 6–5 victory at Murrayfield illustrated the courage and character of a typical Irish side, when, in pre-replacement days, they played with fourteen men for sixty-five minutes after an injury to full back George Norton. Wales, once again, denied them the Triple Crown with a 3–3 draw in Cardiff, the first of many clashes between Kyle and Cliff Morgan. In 1952, the death of George VI caused the English match to be postponed, thereby upsetting the traditional order of games. There had already been signs that the Irish were on the wane when Wales won 14–3 at Lansdowne Road in a match that was to be Mullen's last. The game against England, played in a blizzard, was lost 3–0, and the glory days were over.

The great individual players continued to pop up – Tony O'Reilly was one of the stars of the 1955 Lions' tour to South Africa – but with the game moving ever more steadily towards the ethos of tactics and discipline, the Irish got left behind. They remained the greatest of tourists, however, marked by the number of Irishmen to captain the Lions: Thompson (1955), Dawson (1959), Kiernan (1968), McBride (1974) and

Fergus Slattery

Fitzgerald (1983). Ciaran Fitzgerald, another hooker, led Ireland to their first Triple Crowns since 1949 in 1982 and 1985. Ireland have continued to produce great characters and Lions . . . Moss Keane, Fergus Slattery, Willie Duggan and now Keith Wood, the hooker at the heart of the 1997 British Lions success.

It may be over forty years since he starred with the Lions, but Tony O'Reilly has rarely been out of the news since. His rise to become one of the world's most successful businessmen has been as spectacular as his exploits on the rugby field when he set try-scoring records on his two Lions' tours in 1955 and 1959. Business commitments took their toll, and his rugby career appeared to have ended in 1963 with his twenty-eighth cap for Ireland. However, back he came seven years later when Bill Brown withdrew on the Thursday before the match against England at Twickenham in 1970 and, with the rest of the squad clambering off the bus for training, the O'Reilly Rolls – chauffeur and all – purred into the car park. The media lapped it up.

As O'Reilly got changed before the game, he picked up a telegram sent from former colleague and scrum half Johnny Quirke which read: 'Heinz beanz are haz beanz.' In as much as O'Reilly was scarcely involved in the game at all, Quirke was right, but O'Reilly's one notable moment came when he found the ball rolling towards him, with the England forwards in dangerously close attendance. O'Reilly said: 'I found myself at the last moment reduced to bravery. As I emerged from momentary unconsciousness, I heard a loud (and I must confess, Irish) voice shouting: "And kick his bloody chauffeur while you're at it!"'

CHAPTER 10

FRENCH RESISTANCE

WHEN YOU WATCH the French playing rugby, it is hard to believe that this was a game brought to them by the British. To slip across the Channel is to move from a world of natural reserve and sangfroid to Latin passion and hot blood, where style is every bit as important as substance. From the transport café, the mug of tea and the roll-up, to the pavement baguette, the café cognac and the whiff of Gitanes.

Though an encounter like Brive v Pau can occasionally make Pontypool v Neath resemble a Sunday School friendly, it is in the field of culture that France is best known for its contribution to civilisation. However, when it comes to examining the influence of the likes of Marie Curie, Paul Cézanne and Gustave Eiffel, the Rugby Football Union sees them in slightly less romantic terms – namely, as faces on French banknotes. When the rugby-playing world turned professional in 1995 it was an announcement – so the cynics said – that might have produced a puzzled inquiry from the French Rugby Union. 'Oui, oui, it says here we can pay our players – but is there anything actually new in this idea?'

Before the game went open, the four home unions had long

been concerned – to put it mildly – over what was going on across the Channel. Over there resided the *enfant terrible* of world rugby, capable of magnificent, inspirational play, but tainted by associations of commercialism that they scarcely bothered to conceal. Britain, and the RFU in particular, had a running battle with France for more than half a century over the thorny issue of professionalism – and there was no middle ground between one country for whom blistered feet were the penalty for not removing the 100 franc notes from the boot before taking the field, and another for whom a visit from the tooth fairy was almost enough to get someone banned for life.

The fact that the issue never actually got resolved was more through fear of the French leading a European rugby break-away than any change to the way France went about conducting their internal affairs, not to mention the fact that even the most dyed-in-the-wool RFU zealot would have had to concede that rugby as a whole would have been much the poorer without the uninhibited charm and flair that France brought to the game. There was also the suspicion that the French finally got the International Board off their backs by the simple and time-honoured expedient of inviting them over to Paris for a good old-fashioned piss-up.

Paris has remained the international headquarters of rugby in France, although the strength of its game has always been in the south. It was the British, at Le Havre, who brought the game over the Channel in the early 1870s, and it quickly began to flourish in the southern regions, where workers in the wine trade took to it as naturally as a game of pétanque. Certainly, it was taken up more enthusiastically in the poorer, more rural areas than the richer, industrial north. Nonetheless, when the first club championship was held in 1892, it was not only played in Paris, but the rule was that it could only be won by clubs based in the capital. Inevitably, however, the net was widened to embrace the true rugby heartlands, with Stade Français winning the championship eight times before 1910, and Bordeaux seven times before the Great War.

France also won the rugby gold medal at the 1900 Olympic Games, although the fact that the final was contested by Germany was indicative of the established rugby nations having concluded that the Olympics should be treated as a showpiece springboard for emerging countries rather than a meaningful international event. In 1920 in Antwerp, for example, France finished runners-up, not a great achievement given that only two countries entered, and that the other one was the USA. The Americans retained their Olympic title in 1924, beating France again in the final in Paris by 17–3, and such was the ferocity of the USA tackling, that there was a suspicion that they had brought in several grid-iron players for the occasion. Ironically, this first official inquiry into allegations of professionalism in a match involving France was centred on the opposition, with the decision being that the not so gentle giants in the US team were bona fide union men from Stamford University.

It was not until 1920 that the Fédération Française de Rugby came into existence, by which time the French were well blooded in the international arena. They made their debut in 1906, when Dave Gallaher's All Blacks travelled to the Parc des Princes at the end of their British tour, and however tired and bruised the New Zealanders might have been, a 38–8 defeat was far from a disgrace for the northern hemisphere newcomers.

Before the First World War France played twenty-eight internationals and won just once, against Scotland, 16–15, at the Stade Colombes in 1911. Just before the kick-off, there was still no sign of the French winger Charles Vareilles, and so they pressed the French sprinter, André Franquenelle, who was in the crowd as a supporter, into emergency service. Vareilles did in fact turn up as the team was leaving the dressing room, but they stuck with Franquenelle, who won two more caps. Vareilles never played again. Before the Great War, the French national side – while not quite regarded as a joke on the other side the Channel – was not considered a decent match for any of the established nations, and the victory over Scotland was a bigger shock in its day than when Italy beat the Scots – the then champions – in their first game of the inaugural Six Nations Championship eighty-nine years later.

Another shock to the Scots came two years later with the behaviour of the home crowd. French spectators were already earning a reputation for volatility, and after the Scots had won 21–3, the referee James 'Bim' Baxter was very nearly trampled to death during a crowd riot. The International Board warned the French that 'unless adequate steps are taken to prevent the recurrence of such treatment, international matches with France will have to cease'. The French Union – the Union des Sociétés Françaises de Sport Athlétique – issued an official apology, although the Scots still declined to play them in 1914. Mr Baxter may have been slightly to blame. When the crowd were jeering his decisions, the referee thought they were applauding, so he smiled and started bowing towards them, which made the crowd even more angry.

The popularity of the game in France had spread to such an extent that, by this time, the French were facing the sort of financial problems that had led to the great divide in England. Gate money was flooding in, and a not insubstantial amount of it was finding its way into the players' pockets. And why not, reasoned the French. If the game had actually started in France rather than England, rugby would have been a professional sport right from the outset. Remember, there had been no specific demand for the original game to remain strictly amateur other than by the RFU, whose motives, shall we say, may not have been entirely altruistic. In laying down the law about what was and was not permissible, the RFU kept the game snugly under their own control.

However, it remains unlikely that the French would have got themselves into the amount of trouble they did with the home unions – who knew little of the workings of each other's rugby – had they not flaunted their shamateurism quite so shamelessly. Good players quickly left the smaller clubs for bigger ones, and drifted back and forth between union and league more or less at will. The initial success of the French championship also played a part. Rivalries at club level were far more intense than they were back in Britain, and the corresponding urge to offer inducements to players was nigh on irresistible. There was, in short, no such thing as a friendly in French club rugby, even in those formative years. After initially being confined to Paris, the first truly national club championship was introduced in 1906, which – even though the Border League in Scotland had been going for longer – makes it the oldest club championship in the world.

At the end of the First World War, a conflict which not unnaturally led the Scots to put their 1913 roughing up into a slightly less serious context, Scotland resumed fixtures with the French, and when they headed back to Paris in 1920 it was not so much the mental scars that had failed to heal, as the physical ones from the 1914–18 conflict. While the Scots fielded the one-eyed Jock Wemyss, he of the 'Where's the 1914 jersey we gave you, Jock?' fame, the French side contained a player by the name of M.F. Lubin-Lebrère. He was clearly a resilient type, having had seventeen German bullets removed from his body. It's a good job it didn't rain, otherwise he would have been running around like a human colander.

1920 was an historic year for the French, as they won their first-ever international away from home, against the Irish, and also came close to beating England at Twickenham. France's growing stature as a rugby-playing nation was illustrated by home wins over England in 1929 and 1931, but the chaotic nature of their administration – at least as perceived by the home unions – led in 1931 to them being told to go and play on their own until they sorted themselves out. The Union des Sociétés Françaises de Sport Athlétique was streamlined after the 1913 Scottish riot, but only to the extent of giving themselves a mercifully shorter name, the Fédération

Française de Rugby. But an internal row led to twelve clubs splitting from the Fédération and setting up on their own.

Quite what this internal squabbling had to do with the International Board, who after all had twice declined France's application for membership, is not clear, but with their customary pomposity, the home unions announced on 13 February, 1931 that all French fixtures – club and country – would be abandoned at the end of that season. And so the game against England in April, in which France three times came from behind to win 14–13, marked France's last match in the championship for sixteen years.

This loss of international contact was not as catastrophic as it might have been in other countries. The French had had enough of the IB's Victorian parent attitude and on the back of the huge interest in their own domestic game, took their leave of the home unions with a Gallic shrug of the shoulders and the raising of two fingers. The club championship in France, which already created far more passion and interest than any international in Paris, grew even stronger as a result.

The irony for the International Board was that their decision actually had the opposite effect to the one intended because French domestic rugby now assumed an importance that made semi-professionalism even more prevalent. With nothing else to play for – except to swap comparatively small beer fixtures with Italy, Romania and Germany – the French clubs resorted to the chequebook as never before. The lines of communication to Britain remained open, but the French consistently failed to prove to the IB that their game was even remotely close to tackling the question of financial inducement. The British Establishment, in fact, appeared to be far more concerned with what was going on in French rugby during the 1930s than they did with German politics. If the British government had taken the same stance over Hitler as the IB did over French rugby, the Second World War would have been under way long before 1939. You can imagine the scene down at the East India Club as an RFU official idly flicked past the invasion of Czechoslovakia on the front pages and moved swiftly to the back. 'Shocking news from Europe, Farqharson. The bally French have been paying their rugger chaps again.'

With a deliciously inappropriate sense of timing, the IB finally agreed to a peace treaty with the French a few months before war broke out in Europe. According to the IB, the French had finally confessed that they'd been bending the amateur rules, and they also promised to suspend their club championship, which the IB regarded as being at the root of the monetary evil. Once again, the headmasters of the world game issued one of their periodical lectures on how they expected their pupils to behave. Re-emphasising the word 'amateur' as the underpinning word of the game, they said: 'no player who has been proven guilty of receiving payment, other than actual out-of-pocket travelling and hotel expenses, is ever allowed to play Rugby Football again, or to act in any official capacity in connection with any Rugby Football Club.'

In agreeing to suspend their championship, the French were, it could be said, getting in some useful practice for their next surrender to the German Army, but it was the price laid down for re-admission to mainstream international rugby. The Second World War itself certainly played a big part in the healing process, and an *entente cordiale* match between French and British XVs at the Parc des Princes on 25 February, 1940 was only just squeezed in before rugby was placed on the back burner by events at the Channel port of Dunkirk.

Remarkably enough, the French re-launched their club championship even before the Normandy Landings on D Day, with all the old problems of violence, poaching and paying of players. So why then were matches between France and the home nations resumed, without so much as an admonishing word, in 1947? Well, it might well have been down to the IB deciding to abandon the soap box for a more conciliatory position, or it might, more cynically, have been something to do with the fact that soap boxes – or boxes containing luxuries such as soap – were in extremely short supply in postwar Britain. Rationing in France was abolished far sooner than on the British mainland and, distasteful though it was for IB officials to abandon their principles for a plate of after-match Perigord pigeon, a side order of truffles and a glass or two of vintage champagne, they bravely bit the bullet and decided that the occasional trip to France might now be in order.

However, by 1951 one or two of life's little essentials – such as roast beef and decanters of port – were once again available on the British mainland, as the IB once again began flexing their muscles in France's direction. They wrote reminding them of their conditions for re-entry in 1939, namely the abolition of a championship that by now was not only tainted by money, but so violent as to make referees go in fear of their health, and in some cases, their lives. The French Federation agreed to disband it yet again, but this time the clubs refused. 'Sorry,' the FF told the IB, 'we don't appear to be able to stop them.' 'That's okay,' replied the IB, 'at least you had a jolly good try.' And so the championship was reluctantly sanctioned, with the attendant promise from the FF that this time they really would do their best to keep it within the bounds of propriety. In truth, the IB only had two ways to go this time. Cut the French off again and risk losing all influence in a rugby-expanding Europe, or keep the French onside and maintain their own role as the game's spiritual leaders. Temporarily, at least, the gun went back in the holster.

French rugby made rapid strides after the war, reaching a high point in 1958 when they won a series in South Africa. The captain of that side was Lucien Mias, who had been a member of the side crushed 25–3 by Basil Kenyon's 1951–52 Springboks (a big margin under the old scoring values) and he took the earlier beating badly. Mias won fifteen caps after making his debut in 1951 before spending four years away from rugby to concentrate on his medical studies (which should have been proof to the IB that he wasn't being paid enough). On his return he set about transforming a hugely talented team into a disciplined unit capable of giving more than a hard time to the major rugby powers.

France was already developing an exceptional back row of Guy Basquet, Jean Matheu and Jean 'Monsieur Rugby' Prat, and gained a glimpse of what the team might be capable of when Bob Stuart's All Blacks, beaten only twice in the UK, came to France. The two previous New Zealand visits had both resulted in heavy beatings, but this time Prat scored the try which marked France's greatest rugby achievement to date.

That match was Mias's penultimate game before turning to his medical studies, and the way for his return was paved by an abject French season in 1957, when they not only failed to score a single point in the home internationals, but also struggled to overcome Romania in front of a remarkable 93,000 crowd in Bucharest. Mias's return was marked by an upturn in fortunes the following year, albeit not enough to suggest anything other than a massacre when the side went to South Africa. Michael Celaya was appointed captain, but an injury put Mias in charge, and he quickly demonstrated a natural talent for leadership. He also appeared to have a natural talent for drinking, as his idea of a quick pick-me-up for the second half of the second Test against the Springboks was half a bottle of rum. If that was his prescription for an out-of-sorts patient when he retired to the medical profession, he must have been a popular doctor.

The French, having hung on desperately for a 3–3 draw in the first Springbok Test, clinched the series with a 9–5 win in the second, largely through Mias's inspirational forward play, although in fairness he probably only had to breathe on people for them to fall over. It was the first time that South Africa had lost a home series for sixty years, and after a similar period on the international scene, France at last arrived as a real force when Mias led them to the championship.

Mias later recalled:

When I began playing for France in 1950, we were a collection of captains with no sense of belonging to each other. That really bothered me. French post-war teams were technically good, and in individual terms, very good indeed. But the collective play was poor. There were certain matches when everything worked well and that was marvellous. But there were other occasions when the English, with their solid approach, but sound principles, caused us to lose.

The four years I spent with my medical studies enabled me to sort out my ideas about rugby football, and I felt I wanted to prove them. No one gave us much hope when we left for South Africa. They said we were beaten before we started. We had some problems because the South Africans thought we were a second class team and from time to time we had to prove and demonstrate that we had both physical strength and spirit.

In Mias's case, the spirit was about 50 per cent proof.

Off the field, however, the French were still struggling to win their verbal battles with the IB, and they ran into tough opposition from the Scots in 1953 when the SRU handed back the French team sheet on the grounds that they had spotted a couple of rugby league players. The players were withdrawn, but the Scots later had reason to believe that the French had sneaked through a third. On and on the conflict rumbled, and it was not until 1978 that the French were finally accepted as official members of the International Board. The home unions had by now conceded that no amount of threat and bluster was going to alter French rugby radically, and so it was time for them to join the family, albeit, for a couple of decades more, in the servants' quarters.

The long-term benefits of the final truce are obvious. There is no more thrilling sight in international rugby than a French side in full cry, and at their best, they take the game to new levels of spectator enjoyment. At their most undisciplined, they are a total shower, but there is nothing worse in rugby – or any sport – than total predictability. France were roundly written off as no-hopers in their 1999 World Cup semi-final against New Zealand at Twickenham, only to bury the All Blacks with an irresistible display of attacking rugby.

CHAPTER 11

'BY CHRIST! I'M KILT ENTOIRELY'

Given the fact that the four home unions occasionally found it hard to agree on the time of day, the concept and formation of a unified team drawn from the best players in England, Scotland, Wales and Ireland, was, on the scale of sporting miracles, right up there alongside American astronauts playing golf on the moon, or, more recently, England beating Australia at cricket.

As demonstrated by the French, individual brilliance without the added ingredients of organisation and teamwork was rarely good enough against top-quality opposition, and the throwing together of players, however talented, from different countries for relatively short periods is not an easy trick to make work – different countries, different accents, different cultures. On top of that, rugby has traditionally been a game in which the odds are stacked in favour of the team playing on home territory, and the British Lions – quite apart from the fact that they only play the very best sides in the world – never play at home. The difficulties involved were never better demonstrated than during the 1950s, when a series of multi-talented Lions' sides failed to win a single series victory. They played off-the-cuff, magical rugby at times, but were all too often ground down by opposition with an intimate knowledge of each other's games and tactics. That disappointingly unsuccessful decade held a clear message for the home unions, but it took another ten years and a further trio of defeats before the Lions were finally to turn the corner in 1971.

The ambition for most players starting out on a rugby career is to represent their country, but for many, the winning of a Lions' jersey is something else again. It's a chance to share the unique camaraderie that is an essential part of rugby union's culture, and also to parade their own talents along-side all those great players they would normally expect to line up against rather than with. The very first combined sides were called, not surprisingly in view of the RFU's inflated sense of their own importance, the 'English Rugby Team', latterly becoming known as 'Britain', 'Great Britain' and, finally and officially, the 'British Isles'. However, just as New Zealand, South Africa and Australia naturally evolved into the All Blacks, Springboks and Wallabies, it was inevitable that the combined side would acquire an identity of their own, and for the tour of South Africa in 1924 they inherited the nickname – from the symbol on their tour ties – of 'the Lions'.

Those first teams did not immediately latch on to the famous red jersey, initially kitting themselves, albeit not quite in such garish form as the Harlequins, in various mish-mashes of red, white and blue. The poor old Irish were not even represented until 1930, and then only after they lodged a complaint. The original 1888 team wore the three colours in narrow stripes, with white shorts, and in 1891 switched to red and white shirts with navy shorts. Between the two wars it evolved into a navy jersey with white shorts and red socks, and when Ireland piped up that it was about time a dash of green was added, a dash was all it was. A green flash – the kind normally worn with a kilt – was added to the stockings, and when those were rolled down, all evidence of an Irish connection disappeared.

Junior doctors have their own way of letting the ref know when he's just made an awful decision.

Final of the Hong Kong Rugby Sevens, 1999. Mel Gibson and friend.

1987 World Cup, NZ v Fiji. Try for the skipper. Captain (David) Kirk goes over at warp factor 9.

Lions v NZ Juniors, Wellington, 1977. 'Who was the pillock who wrote that song about mud being glorious?'

ance v England, 1991 World Cup. Brian Moore never had much love for the
ench – or anyone else come to that – and celebrates Carling's try in the quarter
al.

nnis Easby and Carling kiss and make up. In the event of an old fart breaking
t, please leave by the fire exit behind you.

Above: Australia v Canada, 1995 World Cup. David Campese. The goosestep about to lay another golden egg.

Left: World Cup, Group D. Wales v Samoa, October, 1999. Jenkins the boot bangs over another one.

Below left: Martin Johnson during England training with the Royal Marines, July 1999. I Mike Tyson had taken a fancy to this ear, he want it served with cheese sauce.

Below right: England v SA, Twickenham, 1998. Jeremy Guscott, male model and role model.

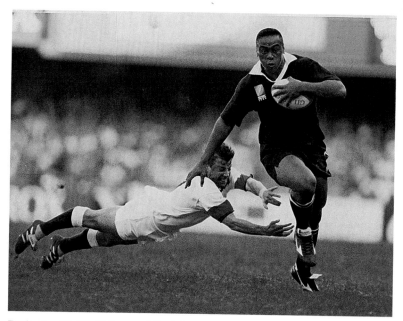

England v NZ, World Cup semi-final Cape Town, 1995. Rob Andrew dives in vain to catch Jonah Lomu and thinks: 'Thank God I missed him.'

England v SA, 1998. Lawrence Dallaglio holds a team talk. 'Now then, lads, if you get a call from the Sunday newspapers, don't say a bloody word.'

1999 World Cup, Wales v Australia. 'Not me, you berk, tackle *him*'. Tim Horan gets away.

World Cup semi-final, 1999. Christian Dominici bursts clear, France v NZ, Twickenham. *Sacre-bleu*! The unthinkable happens to the unbeatable.

Above left: 1995 World Cup final. Number one supporter Nelson Mandela congratulates François Pienaar after South Africa's victory over New Zealand.

Above right: 1999 World Cup final. John Eales holds the trophy aloft on the day Australia decided to maintain the monarchy. 'Thanks, Ma'am, and I did vote for you, honestly.'

1997 Lions v Eastern Province XV, Port Elizabeth. 'Whatever you do, lads, keep your hair on.' Jason Leonard, Keith Wood and Tom Smith.

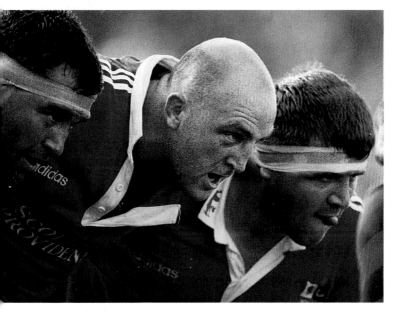

V'aiga Tuigamala. 'Don't look so worried. It's just a little number we knocked up a line-dancing class.'

The origins of the final change were initiated by New Zealand, who complained that the navy blue jerseys against the All Blacks were confusing. Indeed there were a number of instances of disgruntled forwards getting mixed up and bopping their own men. (In actual fact, the Lions' navy blue was the original choice of the New Zealanders, but the Maoris' all-black jerseys had caught the public imagination, and that's what they settled on.) As for the Lions, it was not until 1950 that the strip we know today – red jersey, white shorts and blue socks with a green turnover – became the official British Isles colours.

There was nothing terribly official about any Lions' tour up until then. The original trip – to Australia and New Zealand – in 1888 was organised by a collection of players hoping to make a few quid, and it evolved into a combination of players, private promoters and ad hoc committees set up whenever a tour was proposed. The RFU got involved only to give their blessing/sanction, which they did with the usual issuing of stern reminders about amateur principles. Only in 1949 did the home unions grasp the desirability of adding some proper organisation to the whole thing, which is when they set up the Four Home Unions Tours Committee.

Rugby being the sort of game it was, not everyone could spare the time or the money to spend a great chunk of the summer away from home, with the result that many famous names never appeared in a Lions' jersey. The list includes Billy Bancroft, Arthur Gould, Adrian Stoop, Wavell Wakefield, Ronnie Poulton-Palmer, Wilson Shaw, George Stephenson and Ernie Crawford. And such were the financial problems created by the Great Depression years in the 1930s that the Lions on one occasion selected ninety-five players before reaching the required number of twenty-nine acceptances. Little wonder, in those circumstances, that the list of Lions contains many players who were never actually capped by their country.

It was pretty hard for many to give up their jobs for a tour, however glamorous, and for an expenses allowance of three shillings per day, which was the going rate – paid by the host country – before the First World War. Between the wars it went up to five shillings, and in the 1950s it rocketed up to ten bob. That's fifty pence in today's currency. It was money well spent by the hosts, however, as the Lions invariably dragged in bumper attendances wherever they went.

The original tour, in 1888, was the brainchild of three England internationals – cricketers, as opposed to rugby players. Alfred Shaw, Arthur Shrewsbury and A.E. Stoddart had already toured Australia in a flannelled fool capacity and felt that a muddied oaf visit would go down well. New Zealand came into the trip, but for less than half the matches, and the whole thing was sanctioned by the RFU on the strict understanding that amateur rules were adhered to. This they were, by all accounts, but not before one poor sap, J.P. Clowes, had been removed from the boat just before it sailed on the grounds that he'd been involved in a sponsorship deal with a firm of outfitters. Another hapless wretch was debarred from the Australian leg of the tour for the heinous crime of having discussions – nothing else, just discussions – about a professional switch to Aussie Rules. Now we know where the Ministry of Defence got their 'Walls Have Ears' and 'Careless Talk Costs Lives' poster ideas from in the Second World War.

It is worth recalling also, amidst all the angst today about hectic schedules, that this particular tour was something a bit more than a weekend break. They were away for nine months, played fifty-four matches – nineteen of them under Australian Rules – and had a squad of only twenty-one players. By way of comparison, when England toured South Africa in 2000, they took forty-three players for a total of five games.

However, this was an unofficial visit, and the first official Lions' tour – to South Africa – took place in 1891. Once again, it was the by-product of a previous visit by England's cricket team, the official invitation coming from Western Province, underpinned by financial guarantees from Cecil Rhodes. It was, so to speak, a half-Lions' tour, comprising

English and Scots. In 1896, again to South Africa, it was English and Irish, and in 1908, to New Zealand, an Anglo-Welsh party.

On that first official trip to South Africa, captained by W.E. Maclagan, the combined side conceded one try on the entire tour, and that in the opening match. Maclagan was a ferociously strong man and although another opponent – in the Transvaal game – succeeded in getting over the try line, Maclagan picked him up and dumped him on the 25 yard line. The first Test, in front of a crowd of 6000 at Port Elizabeth, was South Africa's first in international competition.

On the return visit in 1896 more than half the party were Irish, including the legendary Tommy Crean of Dublin Wanderers. Quite a few of the tourists in these early years stayed on as settlers, including Crean. The Irishman joined the Imperial Light Horse regiment, earning his Victoria Cross after coming under attack from a Boer force at Tygerskloof. It was here, after being hit for a second time, that Crean supposedly came out with the immortal line: 'By Christ! I'm kilt entoirely.' When the Lions toured South Africa in 1997, the forwards prepared for the physical confrontation with endless hours on the scrummage machine, which was a far cry from the way Crean's pack got itself into peak condition. The edict he laid down could scarcely have been more strict. 'No man,' he said sternly, 'shall indulge in more than four tumblers of champagne on match days.'

Another VC in that party was Robert Johnson, who, like Crean, played for Dublin Wanderers and joined the Imperial Light Horse. His gong came after leading his men through point-blank fire to take the Boer stronghold at Elandslaagte. Another man in that party to be decorated – with the Military Cross in France during the First World War – was the Rev. M. Mullineux, the Blackheath fly half, who was never capped by his country, despite leading the Lions three years later in 1899.

The 1896 Lions won the series but provided South Africa

with their first-ever international victory in the final Test at
Cape Town. The only score came from a converted try by
Alfred Larard who had played rugby league in the north of
England after the broken-time payments dispute. Had he
remained in England he would have been banned from union,
but the South Africans accepted him back into the amateur
ranks without question when he later emigrated there. It's a
wonder the RFU didn't declare the game, and the result,
invalid.

The 1899 tour to Australia was certainly invalid in terms
of meaningful Lions' history. It was not a representative side,
with the majority of the twenty-one players never having
come remotely close to an international cap. However, it was
a pukka Lions' side that returned to South Africa in 1903,
and it was on this visit that the Springboks first sprang to
prominence as a rugby nation of real substance. Under the
captaincy of D.R. 'Darky' Bedell-Sivright, the Lions lost half
their twenty-two tour matches, drawing the first Test 10–10,
the second 0–0, and losing the third 8–0. South Africa were
not to lose another rugby series against anyone until 1956.

In 1904 the Lions, having won comfortably enough in
Australia, were beaten by the All Blacks in their only Test in
Wellington, and were resoundingly thumped again by the All
Blacks on their 1908 visit, 32–5 and 29–0. They did manage
to draw the second Test 3–3, but only because the home team
had rested several key players. On their 1910 visit to South
Africa the Lions, for the first time, came close to taking a
side that accurately represented the playing strength of British
rugby union.

That was certainly not the case in 1924 for the tour to
South Africa. This tour was a landmark only for giving birth
to the Lions' official name. England and Scotland, the two
sides representing the British Isles that year, had many world-
class players, but very few of them – W.W. Wakefield included
– made the trip. The goalkicker they took with them, full back
Dan Drysdale, did not manage to land a single kick at goal,

and the England forward Tom Voyce, who took over from him, ended up leading points scorer with 37.

There were also a large number of injuries, the first of them before the Lions had even got ashore. The redoubtable Jamie Clinch was appointed tour entertainments officer for the boat journey and, had to be helped from the stage after jarring his spine during a revue that he had both written and produced. It was at about this time that moves were afoot to compensate players for time off work for injuries and things such as providing their own wardrobes. Whatever costume Clinch was wearing on stage when he performed his involuntary double axel, he had almost certainly paid for it himself.

Wales's Rowe Harding wrote: 'People will say that there is no solution possible without breaking the existing amateur rules. In that case, by all means break the rules. Until that is done we had much better abandon these teams abroad; they do no good to British rugby, and they do a great deal of harm to British national popularity.' However, in the climate of the time, Rowe Harding was urinating into a particularly strong wind. The RFU was never going to sanction payment for anything, not even the cost of a splint for anyone toppling off stage and breaking a leg during a shipboard hokey-cokey, and neither were the Lions about to stop touring.

In 1930, the Lions were soundly beaten 3–1 by the All Blacks, despite winning the first Test, on a tour memorable for lacking the usual cordial relations between visitors and hosts. This was largely down to the Lions' manager, James 'Bim' Baxter, the English referee who had almost been torn apart by the French crowd in 1913, and who was again rather fortunate to avoid a premature death on this trip. Baxter was probably a jolly nice chap, but clearly earned his living through some other field than His Majesty's diplomatic corps.

Baxter had a running battle with the NZRFU, starting in the first game when the Wanganui players, as was their custom, left the field for the dressing room at half-time. Baxter lodged an official protest, quoting the regulation: 'no player may leave the field without the referee's permission, which should only be given in exceptional circumstances.' This, however, was pretty mild compared to his performance at dinner, when he mentioned the roving loose forward role made famous by the 1905 All Blacks' captain Dave Gallaher. Baxter got up, called Gallaher (and all who played like him) a 'cheat', and sat down again. Needless to say, a standing ovation was not forthcoming. The rugby players of that era must have been a lot better behaved than in later times because there is no record of Baxter being struck between the eyes by a flying bread roll.

The Lions' approach to that tour, indeed any tour, was hardly what you might describe as a triumph for forward planning. Quite apart from selecting a manager whose major forte appeared to be in verbally abusing his hosts, their captain was selected by Baxter approaching Doug Prentice, just before the ship weighed anchor, with the words, 'Look, Doug, we think you'd better be skipper.'

It was much the same story on the 1938 visit to South Africa. Wilf Wooller, Cliff Jones and Wilson Shaw were just a few of the leading players missing from the squad, and the number one goalkicker and full back Vivian Jenkins sustained an injury in the first Test that led to him missing the remainder of the series.

There was a curious end to an otherwise disappointing tour when the Lions, having won the final Test 21–16, saw their captain Sam Walker carried off the field, shoulder-high, by the home players. You'd be hard pressed to imagine that happening today. Furthermore, the Lions had trailed 13–3 at half-time, and when the result came through on the wires to London, the operator decided that it had somehow got transposed in transmission, and put it out as a Springbok victory. Many a newspaper had been hurled across the breakfast table before the true result was known.

The Lions continued to disappoint during the '50s, starting with a 3–0 defeat in New Zealand after the first Test had ended in a draw. The visitors had breathtaking talent in the backs – Jackie Kyle, Bleddyn Williams, Lewis and Ken Jones, Noel Henderson, Jack Matthews and Rex Willis – but were steamrollered by the All Black forwards. The biggest let down came in the third Test, when New Zealand trailed 3–0 with only thirteen men, but came back to win 6–3. The final game, won by the All Blacks 11–8, was the most thrilling, with Ken Jones scoring one of the great international tries, and Bleddyn Williams looking certain to go over near the end until brought down six inches short by a thunderous tackle from Peter Henderson. It earned Henderson not only the gratitude of a nation, but a few extra quid into the bargain. An English rugby league scout was there with a cheque for £2000 to lure Henderson away to the paid ranks, but the New Zealander's transfer value shot up as a result of saving the game, and he finally agreed to go for £3500.

Bleddyn Williams himself was in no doubt about where British rugby needed to improve in order to put together winning tours in places like New Zealand. 'When we came back from that tour,' he said, 'we preached the gospel around Britain for as long and as hard as we could. We tried to tell people how important it was for a pack to play as a unit like the All Blacks, particularly as far as rucking was concerned.'

Danie Craven described the 1955 Lions side to South Africa – the first ever to travel by air – as 'the strongest touring side I have ever seen here', but a tour that promised so much still ended in relative disappointment. They had, for once, a world-class forward in the second row in Rhys Williams, and their class in the back division was summed up by Tony O'Reilly's description of the centre, W.P.C. Davies, one of the select band of Oxbridge students who never won a Blue but went on to play rugby for their country. 'He threw the pass away like a toffee paper, but if you could catch it you had nothing in front of you but the turnstiles.' And, initially at any rate, it looked as though these Lions had the measure of the Springboks.

The first Test was one of the best ever. The Lions, inspired by a brilliant Cliff Morgan try, led 23–11 early in the second half, but when Theunis Briers dived over in injury time to bring the South Africans to within a point at 23–22, the Lions held their breath as a not too difficult conversion drifted just the wrong side (albeit not for them) of the posts. As the whistle went, Rhys Williams collapsed in a combination of relief and exhaustion. They lost the second Test 25–9 in Cape Town, won the third 9–6 with a rare example of the Lions keeping a game tight, but a combination of injuries and fatigue conspired against them in the final Test, and the series was drawn 2–2. Butterfield recalled: 'We were still four countries (as opposed to a unit) each playing to its own little whims and its own little ways. And we never had enough ball. One thing, though. We did smile.'

If any Lions side looked destined for greatness it was the one that left for New Zealand in 1959 under the captaincy of Ronnie Dawson. The backs again oozed class, and the forwards – with the likes of Rhys Williams, Syd Millar, Bryn Meredith, Ray Prosser, Hughie McLeod and David Marques – were certainly not likely to be intimidated by the All Blacks. They even looked capable of shrugging off the loss of England flanker Peter Robbins, who broke his leg in a bout of horseplay in Newport after the squad was chosen. This tour, though, was not only a tragedy for the Lions – who lost 3–1 in a series that could easily have finished the other way around – but it was not a great one for rugby either because it established the rule of the boot, Don Clarke's boot, to be precise. The Lions scored 165 tries in winning twenty-seven of their thirty-three matches in Australia and New Zealand, but the ones that mattered went the other way. It seemed that they would never find a way of beating the All Blacks, even when they clearly possessed the more talented side.

In the opening Test in Dunedin, the Lions scored four tries to nil, yet still came away on the wrong end of it after Clarke kicked all the All Black points in an 18–17 win. Two of his six penalties from ten attempts were from over fifty yards, and a local newspaper headline summed it up: 'Clarke 18, Lions 17.' The Lions also led in the second Test before Clarke's boot did for them again, and their sense of injustice was further fuelled by an incident early in the second half when, with the Lions leading 6–0, O'Reilly chipped over Clarke's head towards the New Zealand line. Clarke cynically took O'Reilly out, but that earned only a penalty as opposed to a penalty try. The All Blacks pinched it with a late try from Clarke, converted by himself of course, and the Lions left the field feeling that if Clarke couldn't rescue the All Blacks, then the referee would.

There was not much argument about the third Test, when a tremendous All Black performance up front earned them a 22–8 victory, and the largest ever crowd in New Zealand, 63,000, gathered in Auckland to witness the Lions at least get something out of the tour with a consolation victory. Three tries to two Clarke penalties was this time a fair reflection of the two sides. The Lions' style was hugely popular with the crowds, and O'Reilly said of Peter Jackson, 'The New Zealanders loved him so much that the Lions were asked to provide him with a one-wheel cycle and three juggling balls so that he could keep spectators entertained when play was not on his side of the field.' Jackson scored a typically weaving try in that game, which marked the Lions' first win over the All Blacks since 1930. Even then, it could have ended in tears, but Clarke – perhaps overcome by some subconscious feeling of fair play – fluffed a late, and for him comparatively simple, penalty.

The Lions of 1959 had some great characters as well as players. David Marques, who regularly went out wearing pinstripes and a bowler hat, was once asked by a team-mate why, having been battered to the ground in an off the ball incident, he got up and shook the culprit's hand. 'Because,' said Marques, 'I wanted to make him feel a cad.' Then there was Ray Prosser, the blunt-talking prop from Pontypool, who complained to the likes of Andy Mulligan and O'Reilly: 'The trouble with you university blokes is that you keep using all those big words, like "corrugated" and "marmalade".'

Manager Alf Wilson had a smooth line in repartee, which he used to good effect after the Lions had complained about the All Blacks' protective shoulder pads – common today, but not then. Wilson's complaints led to them being banned, except upon production of a medical certificate, which did not prevent thirteen of the opposition players wearing them in a provincial game. The Lions won easily, and when one opponent complained that his own side had been 'terrible', Wilson replied, 'Not at all. I thought you did jolly well, considering you had only two fit men.'

The Lions' record in the '50s, three Test wins and one shared series, was a poor return for the talent at their disposal, yet it was still a golden era for British back play, and the rugby public of South Africa and New Zealand warmed to their entertaining style. Sadly, the Lions' sides of the 1960s were to earn neither their affection nor respect.

CHAPTER 12

THE BOOT BOYS RULE

IF ANY OTHER INTERNATIONAL TEAM attempted to perform a tribal dance before a Test match, it would probably be about as intimidating as the hokey-cokey. However, when the All Blacks do it, you'd never guess that it is actually an elongated Maori ritual which translates into something along the lines of: 'It is death! It is life! One last upward step! Into the sun that shines!' The English version is more likely to reduce the opposition to tears of laughter than trembling fear, but as yet, no one has thought of this as a ruse to make it seem less threatening. Instead, opponents have tried a variety of things – from lining up nose-to-nose to turning their backs – but when the All Blacks are performing the Haka, it is pretty difficult not to feel an air of menace.

In New Zealand, the All Black jersey is far and away the biggest symbol of national identity, and to wear it is to be a hero for life. Ironically, the sale of replica All Black strips is far more lucrative overseas, the widely held theory in New Zealand being that the famous jersey is something that can only be earned as opposed to bought from your local High Street sports shop. For the wearer, it not only means pride, but financial riches – even in the old amateur days. An 'amateur' New Zealand rugby union player once told me that he 'couldn't afford' to make the switch to professional rugby league, by which he meant that the wages on offer there would not even halfway compensate him for the loss of associated income that came from being an All Black.

New Zealand's pride in the All Black jersey was never greater than in the 1960s, particularly when it came to inflicting emotional damage on the home nations. The All Blacks did not merely triumph over British rugby in the '60s, they blew it away on their two tours in 1963/64 and 1967, and in 1966 against the Lions. If the Springboks had established themselves as the leading rugby nation between the wars, and then carried on where they had left off when hostilities ceased, it was not to be very long before the All Black shadow would cover the whole rugby world.

The Springboks once again plunged New Zealanders into a mood of depression and recrimination when they thrashed the 1949 All Blacks 4–0 in South Africa. The All Blacks had some mighty forwards, but technically they were miles behind the Boks, who annihilated them in the scrummage.

Springbok rugby crowds have always reserved a special affection for those forwards who look as though they spend their spare time wrestling wildebeest, and the star of that 1949 side was a huge prop by the name of Okey 'the Ox' Geffin. Geffin had first played against a New Zealand side in a prisoner of war camp in Poland, from which, given his Jewish background, he was fortunate to emerge. The Nazis probably took one look at him and decided to leave well alone. When Geffin came to South Africa after the war, he was called the Ox partly because of his size and partly because he had no Christian names in any event. 'How could I have Christian names?' he joked. 'I was a Jewish boy. It cost me thirty rand to have my birth certificate altered.' But alter it he did, to

Aaron Okey Geffin, and the combination of Geffin and the young Springbok No. 8 Hennie Muller, who harried the All Blacks mercilessly from the base of the scrum, was the axis which rendered that Springbok side unbeatable.

The All Blacks recaptured a bit of pride by defeating the strong Lions side in the 1950 series, but the Springboks quickly reminded them who was top dog, not to mention inflicting further misery on northern hemisphere rugby, by winning thirty of their thirty-one matches in the UK (their one defeat coming against London Counties) in 1951/52. The Scots were singled out for particularly ruthless treatment, going down 44–0, and it was a match that marked the one and only cap for the Scotland winger who later became the long-serving secretary of the International Board, John Hart. Why Hart was singled out was a bit of a mystery, as there was nothing too subtle about the Springbok style, with six of their nine tries coming from the forwards. In later years Danie Craven volunteered the thought – and a pretty alien one at that to a South African rugby man – that the Springboks should have soft-pedalled a bit more in that game at Murrayfield. 'We shouldn't have done that to them,' he said. 'We took away their pride, and left them with nothing.'

Norman Mair, who went on to become one of the most respected rugby writers in the game, could consider himself slightly fortunate to have been dropped for that game. Mair recalled: 'It had the same effect on Scottish rugby as an air crash might have if it had involved the whole national team. It was one of those awful days when everything went wrong.' The beating left a horrible scar, and Scotland were to lose their next seventeen matches, not winning again until 1955. For a nation weaned on stories of Robbie the Bruce's plucky spider, it was a dispiriting sight for the Scots to see their rugby team lose so much heart on the back of one match.

The Springboks of that era were, however, capable of much much more than applying the steamroller up front, and Wales's Bleddyn Williams regarded them as the best international side he had ever seen. Despite Wales giving South Africa the hardest match of their tour, which they won by a narrow 6–3 margin, Williams said: 'The Springboks were prepared to use all the equipment at their disposal, whereas the All Blacks were not.' Williams's point appeared to be reinforced when the All Blacks lost to Wales during their 1953/54 tour, and were also beaten by Cardiff, France and South-West France. Wales's victory was secured by Clem Thomas's celebrated crosskick which Ken Jones latched on to for the winning try, thus making it 3–1 to Wales in the history of matches between the two nations. At the time of writing, it is 14–3 to the All Blacks. Incidentally, on that tour the New Zealand full back Bob Scott made himself available at the last minute, prompting the All Blacks to discard plans to blood a young tyro who was making a name for himself as a kicker in provincial rugby. However, the Springboks were not so fortunate on their 1956 tour to New Zealand, running into the kicking machine by the name of Don Clarke who, as we have seen, laid waste the 1959 Lions. It was not as if the Springboks were not warned. Waikato beat the tourists 14–10 in their opening match, in which Clarke landed a penalty, a conversion and a huge dropped goal. Even so, it was not enough to earn Clarke a Test place until the third match, with the series tied at 1–1.

The old adage about making sure you gave away your penalties well out of kicking range did not apply with Clarke around, and an early fifty-yarder set the All Blacks on their way in the last Test to a series-clinching 17–10 victory. It was back row forward Peter Jones, scorer of the decisive try, who summed up the savage nature of All Black–Springbok battles when asked by a radio interviewer afterwards how he felt. 'Absolutely buggered,' said Jones.

The Springboks had been beaten in a series for the first time since 1896, and the balance of power had seemingly shifted to New Zealand.

The Springboks briefly regained top spot in 1960 when, having lost at home to France two years earlier, they won the final Test 8–3 to take the next All Black series, and most of that successful team made the following winter's trip – the last by boat – to Britain. Their only defeat in thirty-four matches was in the final game against the Barbarians, who, for once, placed a higher premium on victory than their traditional attacking principles. This was no showpiece, and the most memorable moment was full back Haydn Mainwaring's demonstration of the benefits of Royal Marine training with a head-on tackle that laid out the South African skipper, Avril Malan.

South Africa, with scrum half Dawie de Villiers and loose forward Frik du Preez emerging as world-class players, saw off the 1962 Lions with minimal inconvenience, but by then the All Blacks were emerging from a period of transition, and boasted giants of their own in Wilson Whineray – who captained the All Blacks in sixty-eight of his seventy-seven appearances – and a colossus of a farmer by the name of Colin Meads.

There were stories of Meads training by running up hills with a sheep under each arm. He played a Test in South Africa with a broken arm, and declined to remain sidelined for the length of time deemed advisable by his doctors after breaking a vertebrae and several ribs in a car crash. Meads was a giant, and a not very gentle one at that. Grabbing hold of Australian scrum half Ken Catchpole by the leg, when the other was trapped, was a bit like pulling the wishbone on a Sunday lunchtime chicken, and it ended Catchpole's career. Meads broke the jaw of Welsh hooker Jeff Young in 1969, and three years earlier laid out the Lions' fly half David Watkins. When one of the Lions' forwards demanded to know why he didn't pick on someone his own size, notwithstanding the fact that there was no one else his own size, Meads replied that Watkins had hit him first. 'Where?' the forward wanted to know, seeing no physical evidence of this unlikely happening. 'On the knee,' replied Meads, with no apparent hint of a smile.

The Springbok centre John Gainsford recalled an incident

in the 1965 series with the All Blacks when, incandescent at some act of thuggery from Meads, he ran the length of the field and jumped on Meads' back as he lay on the ground, thumping him with both fists. Meads felt something landing on his back (he probably thought it had started to rain) and caught hold of his attacker's wrists in what Gainsford described as a vice-like grip. 'He started to laugh, and said: "Now you know what Test rugby is all about, son."'

Remarkably, only one referee ever felt obliged to invite Meads to leave the field, and that was for one of his milder offences against Scotland in 1967. He lunged with his boot at fly half David Chisholm as the Scot gathered a loose ball, and the Irish official, Kevin Kelleher, deemed it to be dangerous play on the grounds that Meads didn't much care whether his boot made contact with the ball, Chisholm or both. Most people felt that, mild offence or not, it was about time previous sins caught up with him. And in any event, Kelleher had already given him an earlier warning. Meads said, 'As I walked off, I was conscious of the crowd booing me, and I thought "I'd like to get hold of you." Mostly, though, I had this terrible feeling of shame. "That's the end," I thought. "That's finished everything."'

However, the New Zealand management gave a clear indication of what they thought of the dismissal, choosing him for the next tour fixture before the disciplinary hearing, although their faces must have turned a mild shade of red at the thought that they themselves had been responsible for choosing Kelleher to referee the game. The All Blacks were so organised in their abuse of the line-out laws that most officials let them get away with it, but with Paddy D'Arcy having penalised them heavily in one of the provincial games, they picked Kelleher ahead of him on the grounds that he would be a softer touch.

After Meads and Whineray came some more famous names – Stan Meads, Colin's brother, Ken Gray, Kelvin Tremain, Brian Lochore, Waka Nathan, Chris Laidlaw, Sid Going and Earle

Kirton. And on top of all this talent, they had the incomparable Clarke to kick their goals. It was Clarke who denied England a deserved draw on their 1963 tour to New Zealand when the full back marked ten yards inside his own half and dummied to kick for goal. England charged him, which under the regulations allowed Clarke to place the ball. This he did, and duly landed it to give his team a 9–6 victory.

> *Welsh supporters are one-eyed and Welsh players are cheats.*
>
> SID GOING, New Zealand scrum-half, 1974

When the All Blacks came to Britain in 1963, the thing they were most vividly remembered for was the ruck. Whether or not the farmers among them used this method for baling hay, the New Zealand ruck might well have provided the idea for the threshing machine, so brutal was it. Opponents would be churned out like barley flying into a hopper, with a marauding band of seventeen-stone Fred Astaires charging into the pile-up. Crash tackling centres such as Ian McRae would charge through, committing two or three tacklers, and by the time the All Black forwards had finished, not many defenders were left to guard the try-line. The outcry was predictable, but very few serious injuries were caused by these skirmishes, and the more sensible opponents quickly learned to get out of the way after going to ground.

It was the most effective way of preventing players from killing the ball, and if the All Black studs failed to get the message across, the resultant penalty and Clarke's right boot were almost as effective. It was simple, direct rugby, and few countries were able to live with it in that era. The only side who managed to stop the All Blacks' rucking style, with the referee's assistance, was Newport. They won 3–0 at Rodney

Parade through a Dick Uzzell dropped goal. The real hero, though, and very nearly a posthumous one, was Glyn Davidge, who had barely a layer of skin left on his back after spending most of the eighty minutes lying over the ball. 'They could kick me as much as they liked,' said Davidge afterwards. 'We won, didn't we?'

Despite the rucking, Whineray's side was immensely popular, and the biggest cheer of the tour was reserved for the All Blacks' captain breaking clear from thirty yards out in the final game against the Baa-Baas, throwing an outrageous dummy, and touching down near the posts. The All Blacks won 36–3 against a Barbarian side who this time – having been heavily criticised for abandoning their attacking traditions against the Springboks – tried to open it out, but rarely had any ball with which to do so. Ironically, the Barbarians only points came from a dropped goal from Don Clarke's brother, Ian, a prop forward. The Barbarians' tradition had begun in 1948 against the Australians in what was essentially a hastily arranged fund-raising match when the tourists informed their hosts that they were short of money to get home. They were usually representative of the very best individual players in Britain, but without the organisation and teamwork to compete with sides as complete as Whineray's All Blacks.

By the mid-60s, southern hemisphere rivalry had expanded to include Australia, whose arrival as a force to be respected came with a drawn series in South Africa in 1965 – an achievement that had thus far been beyond even the All Blacks. The Australian captain was a prop, John Thornett, who organised the Wallaby pack into an effective unit, and their cutting edge in the backs was provided by scrum half Ken Catchpole. The 1960s was a golden era for scrum halves, with Going, Laidlaw, de Villiers and Edwards, but many rated Catchpole the best of them all. His main weapon was the phenomenal speed of his pass, with absolutely no wind-up. In terms of quality of service, his fly half Phil Hawthorne must have felt like a country squire receiving the morning post from his butler.

At the same time as Australia's surge to prominence, the South Africans were starting to travel backwards. On a five-game tour of Scotland and Ireland, they didn't win a single one, and when they then headed for Australia and New Zealand, the Springboks were beaten in five of their six Tests.

139

There was some consolation for them in the third Test at Christchurch when lock Tiny Naude won them the game with a difficult penalty out of thick mud, but the international picture was about to get a good bit muddier than that.

During that tour, the South African prime minister Dr H.F. Verwoerd announced that any All Black team coming to that country would have to be all-white. With a particularly loathsome P.S., he specifically singled out Maoris, and New Zealand did the civilised world a favour by informing the doctor exactly where he could stick the proposed tour of 1967. And so Brian Lochore's All Blacks came to Britain instead.

A year earlier, Michael Campbell-Lamerton's British Lions had been no match for New Zealand, and the Scottish forward had even stood himself down twice from the Test side. When they started off in Australia, winning the second Test 31–0, it had looked pretty promising for the Lions, who had their usual vintage collection of backs with the likes of David Watkins, Mike Gibson and Dewi Bebb. However, the Lions were already starting to show signs of internal disharmony, thanks to Campbell-Lamerton's unwillingness to recognise the authority of the assistant manager, a coach in all but name, John Robins. Campbell-Lamerton had been a compromise choice as captain ahead of Alun Pask, but by insisting on retaining the absolute control of previous Lions' captains, he effectively declined to recognise Robins' appointment. The playing party split into various factions, and the second ingredient in the Lions' 1966 downfall in New Zealand was their mistake in trying to take on the All Blacks up front. Against an All Black pack with the Meads brothers in the second row, and a back row of Nathan, Lochore and Tremain, it was the equivalent of attempting to break into Fort Knox with a hat pin.

It was no surprise when Lochore's side proved unbeatable in Britain in 1967, on a tour cut short because of an outbreak of foot-and-mouth disease (among the cattle rather than the players) in Ireland.

Curiously, the All Blacks had had internal divisions on this trip, with the coach Freddie 'the Needle' Allen wanting to play a more expansive game than was their custom. Meads, in particular, took a lot of persuading. The All Blacks, in fact, compromised, altering their style from game to game, largely depending on who they picked at scrum half. Chris Laidlaw, with his elegant spin pass, was a backs' man, while Sid Going, essentially a base-of-the-scrum sniper, was held in rather deeper affection by the likes of Meads. Either way, it didn't seem to matter, with the All Blacks winning fourteen of their fifteen games and drawing the other one against East Wales.

Earle Kirton, at fly half, had not enjoyed a great tour in 1963/64, but he flourished on this trip, as did Fergie McCormack at full back. They beat England (18 points in the first half an hour), Scotland and Wales with studied comfort, and also saw off France. And with all due respect to the Irish, they were also the first All Black side ever to be denied a Grand Slam by herds of cattle foaming at the mouth. East Wales surprised a side lacking a few injured regulars, but the home team – with Gareth Edwards, Barry John, John Dawes and Gerald Davies in the back division – was hardly short on talent, and almost pulled off a notable victory. In the next game, the last, the Barbarians should have won. They missed a simple penalty when leading 6–3, and at 6–6 a missed touch allowed the All Blacks the chance of a counterattack and the winning try.

One beneficial side-effect from the hasty arrangement of this trip was the realisation that major tours did not have to last as long as a pregnancy (nine months was not unusual in rugby's early days) nor did they have to cram in twenty-five to thirty matches. They could, in fact, be trimmed quite appreciably, and the fact that the England match was New Zealand's fourth on tour proved that the long-held notion of a side requiring a dozen warm-up matches under their belt was wholly outdated, at least for one-nation sides. The Lions, with groups of players coming together for the first time, certainly needed a slightly longer build-up.

Another benefit from the Lochore tour was that the home nations were at last appearing to absorb the lessons of the All Blacks' fast, direct style, and assimilate it into their own rugby. The southern hemisphere had been on top for long enough, and it was to be the British Lions who redressed the balance of power in the next decade.

CHAPTER 13

RED ALL OVER

THERE HAS PROBABLY NEVER BEEN a more evocative sound in rugby than that of the Welsh crowd in full voice, and during the late '60s and throughout the '70s, they were fed the opportunities until they wanted no more – burst their braces, in fact. Up and down the valleys of the Principality, the bakers' vans were on double time delivering loaf after loaf of heavenly bread, and a friend of mine from Wales used to deliver a gloating message every time his team triumphed over the English. He eventually gave up on the grounds that it had long since lost any semblance of novelty value – like telling the same joke every night down at the local.

To the Welsh of that era, the Arms Park (the official title of National Stadium never quite stuck) was to rugby folk what Lourdes was to religious pilgrims. Life was still harsh in the valleys, where rattling coughs in the working men's clubs and miners' institutes were the inevitable by-product of life at the coal face, but where life was also enriched by joyously recounting the exploits of those players destined to become rugby legends. The Welsh team of that era gave the country an indelible identity – not to mention launching an entire career for Max Boyce.

Wales did not manage to win a single Triple Crown between

1911 and 1950, and even when they provided some of the truly great players of the Lions sides of the '50s – Bleddyn Williams, Lewis Jones, Cliff Morgan, Rhys Williams, Ken Jones – real success continued to elude both them and the Lions. It was a reminder that sparkling individuals were not, by themselves, enough to overcome well-drilled opposition, and the installation of a serious coaching structure for the first time was the vehicle which allowed that group of hyper-talented individuals to turn Wales into a consistently immovable object rather than an occasionally irresistible force. And that influence spread, allowing the Lions to flourish on the world stage as never before.

The 1966 Lions tour to New Zealand was, not to put too fine a point on it, a bit of a shambles, with the captain and coach at constant loggerheads, and the squad split into so many disparate factions that the manager's report contained the recommendation that the Welsh should no longer be allowed to room together. The 1968 Lions tour to South Africa was not much better, the tourists proving to be a highly drilled and dangerous bunch of customers – but only in the art of wrecking hotel rooms. In those days, rugby players were perceived to be slightly peculiar if they failed to leave a club-house, hotel or hostelry looking as though it just been visited by Hurricane Hugo, but that 1968 side sailed completely over the top. They were, to an extent, aided and abetted by the travelling media, who in those days were more like war correspondents – declining to file any stories which might have been regarded as non-conducive to good morale back at home. Just the boys having a bit of fun was the message, as yet another South African hotel manager surveyed what appeared to be the remnants of the Reichstag after a visit from a wartime squadron of B52s.

The South Africans were not impressed with their visitors, either on or off the field. The 1968 Test series was lost 3–0, with one draw, and British rugby was once again shown to be light years behind the southern hemisphere in terms of organisation and a ruthless cutting edge. This was largely down to the quality of domestic rugby, which bred a culture in which a hairy-arsed prop dropping his trousers in the bar was far more in keeping with the spirit of the game than anything quite so vulgar as playing to win.

The RFU, as usual, was behind this 'Play up, play the game, jolly good show, and send us the bill for the damages' attitude, intent as they were on stamping out anything that could be construed as remotely competitive. All domestic games were 'friendlies', not least the appallingly anachronistic county championship which, as far as the RFU was concerned, was a small price to pay for keeping the established order. Anyone who thought that rugby would be best served by engendering a culture of true competition could bugger off and play for Hull Kingston Rovers.

In 1969, Wales went to New Zealand. It was a suicidal itinerary, once again devised by people more intent on flying the colonial flag than lowering opposition colours on the field, with one of the two Tests scheduled a few days after a twenty-six-hour flight. Wales were walloped and there was no hint that the great All Black side of that era was reaching the end of its shelf life.

The fact that Wales had taken the Triple Crown in 1965 was perhaps of less significance than their Under-15 team winning their own version the previous winter. That side included an A. Martin in the pack, a P. Bennett of Llanelli at fly half, and a J. Williams (not quite as distinctive as when he later added his other initials, P.R.) of Bridgend at full back. And 1964 was also to mark the start of another highly significant event in Welsh rugby. Wales's 24–3 defeat by South Africa at Durban on a short tour there precipitated a coaching revolution.

At the WRU annual meeting in Porthcawl, Elvet Jones, a member of the 1938 British Lions, complained that not enough attention was being paid to coaching, proffering the opinion that there was too much concentration on physical fitness at the expense of basic skills and tactics. He added: – 'Rugby at international and club level has deteriorated, and even international players lack the ability to handle the ball properly.' Jones urged a revamping of the coaching committee and the appointment of a national coach, 'lest the AGM of the WRU degenerate into a meeting of social, rather than rugby, clubs'. They heeded his words, and Welsh rugby began to blossom under their coaching organiser, Ray Williams. By 1971 Wales had clinched their first Grand Slam for nineteen years, and thirteen members of that side were to tour New Zealand that summer with the British Lions. A year earlier, Wales had also opened their impressive new National Stadium, thereby doing away with the lottery that constituted any match at the Arms Park, where the River Taff lay above the level of the pitch when the weather was bad.

Another man who was heavily involved throughout this transformation was Clive Rowlands, who played fourteen times for Wales between 1963 and 1965, each time as captain, not that Rowlands advanced the cause of rugby union as a spectator game very much. The Welsh scrum half's idea of spectator involvement was to boot the ball into their midst as often as he possibly could, and quite why people should still be buying Mogadon from Boots when a video of Rowlands' performance at Murrayfield in 1963 is available, heaven only knows. As mastermind of Wales's first win in Scotland for a decade (by a penalty and a dropped goal to nil) Rowlands' constant working of the touchline resulted in 111 line-outs. It is perhaps the most boggling statistic in the entire history of rugby union. Outside Rowlands was David Watkins, who presumably brought along a good book with which to pass the time, but whose skills were such that he was lured north by what was then big money – £16,000 – from Salford. He eventually proved to be a bargain buy, although northern suspicions of southern namby-pambies were aroused in Watkins' debut when he missed a couple of early tackles. 'For Christ's sake, Watkins,' came a cry from the crowd, 'hit him with your wallet!'

1967 was an eventful year for Wales. Gareth Owen Edwards made his debut in Paris, a few months after Gerald Davies and Barry John had made their first appearances against Australia. Delme Thomas, Dai Morris and John Taylor all appeared in the pack for the first time that season, but the debut of all debuts belonged to Keith Jarrett, who had left Monmouth School four months earlier. Jarrett had been making quite an impact as a centre for Newport, but the Welsh selectors were having a hard time filling the No. 15 jersey, and a week before the home game with England, they asked Newport to give him a try at full back. Newport, somewhat unpatriotically, declined, but when Wales picked Jarrett anyway, they decided to relent and give him a go against Newbridge. As it turned out, Jarrett was so awful that he was switched back to centre at half-time.

However, the Welsh selectors' hunch turned into a fairy-tale when Jarrett scored a record-equalling 19 points, including a breathtaking try, as Wales won 34–21. Remarkably, it was only the second try ever scored by a Welsh full back – the first coming from Vivian Jenkins against Ireland in 1934 – and it began when England centre Colin MacFadyean attempted to find a long touch near halfway on the open side of the field. Jarrett charged up to meet it at full speed and, had it bounced awkwardly, he might have ended up looking a total buffoon. However, the ball sat up so perfectly that Jarrett was not even obliged to change gear, and he kept on running to score in the left-hand corner. He added the conversion from the touchline.

Needless to say, the celebrations were not of a restrained nature, and the story goes that Jarrett wandered into the Cardiff bus depot in the early hours of the following morning trying to get home, if indeed he could remember where home was. A bus conductor took pity on him and brought out a vehicle that had long since been put away for the night, whereupon the inspector came out and gave the conductor a bollocking, not for getting a bus out but for getting out a single-decker. 'Get him a double-decker,' he barked. 'Mr Jarrett might want to go upstairs for a smoke.' Jarrett's miraculous introduction turned out to be a bit of a false dawn. He struggled at full back, ended up in the centre, and two years later took the Watkins route to the professional game up north.

Meantime, off the field, Ray Williams had been appointed coaching director, the first post of its kind in the world. Williams had been an outside half for London Welsh, Northampton and Moseley but, like Carwyn James, had the misfortune to be around at the same time as Cliff Morgan. However, competing with Morgan was a doddle by comparison with having to get past the prejudices of those WRU committee men for whom coaching was something akin to medieval witchcraft, and the fact that he had come from a job in the middle of England meant that his arrival was greeted with something approaching hostility by those he was supposed to be working with.

Williams knew this better than anyone and at the AGM, he declined to deliver the customary platitudinous address. 'I am not naïve enough,' said Williams, 'to think that everyone at this gathering is one hundred per cent in favour of coaching. Part of my job is to convince everyone that coaching is in the best interests of the game. Make no mistake, gentlemen, I intend to convince you.' One important aspect of Williams's suitability for the job was that he could handle and manipulate committees. There was a committee for everything in rugby at that time, and Williams knew that he had to get them onside to make it all work.

When Wales lost those two Tests in New Zealand, the doubters were not slow to round on the new man, but Williams had an important supporter in Cliff Jones, chairman of the coaching committee. At the 1969 AGM, Jones pointed out that losing to the All Blacks was merely indicative of the work that needed to be done. 'Moment of truth' is how he described it, adding that the goal now was 'to emerge not as second-class New Zealanders, but as first-class Welshmen'. Whatever that meant.

Wales were able to measure the progress they were making when the South Africans toured the following winter and, although a 6–6 draw meant Wales would have to wait almost another thirty years before finally beating the Springboks, it was a reasonable indication of an upward graph. However, the tour was also being measured by many for the progress – or the lack of it – being made by South Africa as members of the human race. The South African cricket tour had been cancelled and, although the rugby tour went ahead, it was covered as heavily on the front pages as in the sports columns. Ugly scenes in the match at Swansea led to barbed wire barricades around the Arms Park touchlines for the Wales game, although far enough away for Gareth Edwards to dive full length for a mud-splattered equalising try in the corner without shredding several layers of skin. Phil Bennett and Barry John were both in the Welsh side that afternoon, Bennett on the left wing, and it was his long infield pass that allowed John to punt across field for the Edwards try.

John Taylor was not in the side, having withdrawn as part of the anti-apartheid protest, but the great Welsh team of the '70s was already falling into place with the likes of Taylor, Barry Llewelyn, Mervyn and Gerald Davies, John Dawes and J.P.R. Williams, who had made his debut at Murrayfield in 1969, aged nineteen. His vibrant counter-attacking style was made for the new law militating against kicking directly into touch from outside the 22.

You have to respect the opposition. Even if you win by 100 points it's not their fault they're on the field. I still want to have a drink with them afterwards.

BARRY JOHN, Wales back, 1971

With such an array of talent, it was no surprise when Wales
won the Grand Slam in 1971, but it was a vintage championship that year, and the Welsh had to draw on reserves of
courage and commitment as well as skill in order to win it.
They began well enough with a 22–6 win over England
(regaining for them the lead in the series between the two
countries), although at a cost of a depressed fracture of the
right cheekbone for Williams. It was not, however, anything
England could claim the credit for, Williams's injury resulting
from a shuddering collision with Edwards. JPR, interestingly
enough for someone training to be a surgeon, once declared
in an article for the *Sunday Times* that 'pain is emotional',
and he certainly didn't seem to feel any during his playing
days. The Welsh full back was as hard as teak, and when he
ended up in hospital after his sports car was in collision with
a tanker on the M4, a hospital spokesman is alleged to have
said that 'the tanker spent a comfortable night'.

There was a good deal more drama in the next game at
Murrayfield, where the lead changed hands six times, and if
the Scotland captain Peter Brown had converted Chris Rea's
try near the posts five minutes from time, instead of hitting
an upright, it would have left the Welsh requiring two scores.
Gerald Davies, though, brought Wales to within a point with
a last-minute try in the right-hand corner, and when John
Taylor landed the goal from the right touchline, the Welsh
described it as 'the greatest conversion since St Paul'.

Wales, rather than take the road to Damascus, returned to
Cardiff and clinched the Triple Crown with a 23–9 victory
against Ireland before going on to win in Paris for the first
time in fourteen years. It was not a game for the faint-hearted,
and even Barry John, who normally took the view that bodily
contact was not in the interests of either himself or his team,
laid his body on the line for the cause. John's nose was broken
in bringing down Benoit Dauga, and he then went through
for the winning try after Edwards had earlier finished off
JPR's interception near his own line. Just before that game

J.P.R. Williams

the Lions party was announced, and with Llewelyn and Jeff Young unavailable, only Denzil Williams and Dai Morris were not picked from the Welsh side.

The 1971 Lions left for New Zealand with the record of not having won in the southern hemisphere in the twentieth century, but they had at least learned the lessons of the '60s in appointing a talented, complementary management team of Doug Smith, a blunt-speaking Scottish doctor and a 1950 Lion, and Carwyn James, whose international record of two caps for Wales was the legacy of finding himself in direct competition with Cliff Morgan. But James was a rugby coach and a man of rare quality; he was never to take charge of his country's rugby fortunes as the WRU refused to allow him sole charge, but his time with the Lions demonstrated his powers as a rugby thinker and innovator.

The captain was the man who had led Wales to that 1971 Grand Slam, John Dawes, a real players' player whose contribution was not always fully appreciated by Welsh crowds. When he was dropped, the Welsh winger Stuart Watkins gave his own assessment of Dawes' worth. 'If anyone is starting a fund to get John Dawes back into this Welsh team, the first pound comes from me, and the next fifty quid comes from the next fifty wingers in Wales.'

It was the team manager, Dr Doug Smith, who predicted that the series would end 2–1 to the Lions with one draw, and after the tour was over Edwards joked about how difficult it had been to draw that final Test to keep the Doc happy. It was a remarkable achievement. While the All Blacks were by now past their peak, they were even more intense and physical than normal under the captaincy of Colin Meads.

The All Blacks did not much care for the idea of coming second, certainly not at home, and certainly not against the British. But this Lions side had mentally prepared themselves for the inevitable physical contest, and they were ready for the battle. There were scarcely enough stretchers to go round during the infamous Battle of Canterbury which, one week before the first Test, left three Lions so badly injured they were forced to return home. They were the two likely Test props, Ray McLoughlin and Sandy Carmichael, and Irish flanker Mick Hipwell. After the game the Canterbury coach predicted that the Test would be 'like Passchendaele'. Carwyn James was incensed by what he considered to be the All Blacks' policy of what they couldn't beat they might as well flatten, but it was to be tactical nous rather than physical skulduggery which proved decisive in that first Test.

Having hitherto run the ball from everywhere, the Lions put all their eggs for this one in Barry John's tactical kicking basket. John teased and taunted the All Black full back Fergie McCormick with such a masterful display the home selectors – much to the delight of James – subsequently dropped far and away the best No. 15 in New Zealand. Even so, it was only Ian 'Mighty Mouse' McLauchlan charging down a clearance and falling on the ball for the only try that gave the Lions' victory, 9–3, and so exhausted were they from having to repel wave after wave of All Black attacks that not even the Lions were confident of going on to win the series.

Get your retaliation in first.

CARWYN JAMES, British Lions coach, 1971

Sure enough, the All Blacks levelled the series with a 22–12 win, but James said it was that Test – rather than the first one – which convinced him that the Lions would go on to win. The tourists this time not only held their own in the forward battle but, if anything, were slightly the more powerful, and when the Lions won at least an equal amount of possession in the third Test, they virtually won it with a 13-point blitz in the opening quarter. The series was clinched with a 14–14 draw in the final game, thanks to a second half dropped goal from J.P.R. Williams.

Meads was gracious in defeat, singling out No. 8 Mervyn Davies as the key Lions player, but in some ways the Lions had conned the All Blacks with a far more conservative style of rugby in the Tests. Gerald Davies felt that New Zealand were ripe for exposing in that final game, and called for a reversion to the fluent back play which marked their provincial matches, but he was outvoted by those in the squad (i.e. most of them) who felt that winning the series was too important to risk with such a gamble. Davies, a centre for the 1968 Lions, had moved to the wing by then, and thrived on the opportunities carved out by his centres, Mike Gibson and John Dawes, and the counter-attacking style of J.P.R. Williams. One of the tries of the tour was scored by Davies in the second Test after one such thrust from deep in his own half by Williams.

An extra bonus for the Lions was the goal-kicking of John, whose round-the-corner soccer style was only just starting to catch on against the more traditional toe-end method. At the start of the 1971 championship, John had not even been Wales's first choice kicker (JPR was elected for the England game) but his unflappable temperament made him an ideal choice in games of such intensity. He even experimented with a toe-ender in the early stages of the final Test, much to the consternation of his team-mates, but after missing with it, went back round-the-corner as if nothing had happened. John had been injured with the Lions in 1968 but, although there was no doubt that the All Blacks were keen for something similar to happen to him in 1971, he somehow survived the series. The New Zealand flankers launched themselves at him, but mostly found that they were tackling thin air, and one said afterwards: 'He only had to roll his eyes to send me the wrong way.' John played one more season, then retired at the age of twenty-seven.

The nucleus of that team was still there for the 1974 Lions tour to South Africa, even though Gerald Davies, David

Duckham and Gibson were unavailable, but by this time the Lions' strength had shifted emphatically to the forwards, where McLauchlan, Mervyn Davies, Fergus Slattery and Gordon Brown were feared opponents. Added to them were newcomers Peter Wheeler, Fran Cotton and Roger Uttley, along with the old warhorse and captain, Willie John McBride, making his fifth Lions tour.

However, if the emphasis had shifted to the pack three years later, the tactical plan for dealing with physical intimidation had not, and this time the Lions had refined it in the shape of the '99' call – if someone was getting thumped, everyone would join in. It was essentially a device to avoid the danger of players getting singled out and sent off, and it sparked off scenes that almost caused the highlights back at home to be screened after the nine o'clock watershed.

JPR recalled afterwards that there was a feeling that the Springboks regarded the Lions as 'good, but maybe short of bottle'. And Gordon Brown remembers the ugly atmosphere before the third Test in Port Elizabeth, scene of one of the bloodier battles. 'We ran out on to the pitch, and it was ages before the Springboks joined us. They were 2–0 down, and it turned out that their pre-match talk had been given by their Minister of Sport. Can you believe that? Anyway, when the Minister had finished talking to them, you've never seen a side so psyched up.'

It made no difference. Brown ('Broon from Troon') crashed over from a line-out just before the break and South Africa were beaten; the Lions were 3–0 up in the series and, in all honesty, the Springboks were humiliated rather than simply beaten. The Lions had their critics, particularly for playing ten-man rugby when they had so much of the ball, but they had a game plan, and stuck to it rigidly. Even when Mike Gibson came out as a replacement for Alan Old, he could not find a way into the Test team. McBride and his manager, Syd Millar, had decided on their strategy and were not going to be swayed by one individual, no matter how talented.

Willie John McBride

The celebrations after that third Test probably had a bearing on the Lions only managing to draw the fourth. The party was so wild, with hooker Bobby Windsor lighting fires on tables, that the hotel manager knocked on McBride's door and informed him that he was about to call the police. 'Really?' said McBride, who was dressed only in underpants and puffing on his pipe. 'And how many of them do you think there will be?'

The final Test finished 13–13, although the Lions claimed victory when Slattery charged over the line for what appeared to be the winning try. The referee gave a five-yard scrum instead. Phil Bennett said, 'I could see the ref think about giving it, and then thinking to himself, "Hang on. I've got to live in South Africa when these buggers have all gone home."' And when they did get home, all those politicians who had complained beforehand about their visit offering succour to the apartheid regime, were knocking each other over in the rush to have their pictures taken alongside them.

Those Lions successes sadly did not rub off on the 1977 and 1980 sides to New Zealand and South Africa. Both could have been won. Both were lost, 3–1. In '77, they were bogged down in the mud of an atrocious winter – England hooker Peter Wheeler wrote on a postcard home: 'It only rained twice last week, once for three days and the other time for four' – and were tagged 'Lousy Lovers', while in '80, the injury count was off the scale. However, winning the final Test in 1980 was especially memorable for John Robbie, who was playing in his only match for the Lions after seventeen games for Ireland in which he didn't once feature on the winning side.

The Welsh bandwagon, however, rolled on throughout the '70s, including another Grand Slam in 1976 when JPR shoulder charged Gourdon into touch minutes from the end of an epic game with France. Edwards was magnificent throughout that period, establishing himself as probably the greatest scrum half in rugby history, not to mention the strongest. His fifty-three caps were all won in succession – never missing a game through injury between 1967 and 1978 (another Grand Slam season) – and Wales were beaten only once in Cardiff when he was playing. During a Welsh scrum practice under John Dawes, the Welsh coach proposed a code. If Edwards called a word starting with a P it was for the (Pontypool) flanker to break away from the side of the scrum and if it was an S it was for the right (Swansea) flanker to go. Edwards put in the ball and called 'Psychology' – both flankers stayed down.

Edwards partnered just four fly halves for Wales in all that time . . . Watkins (2), Bennett (24), John Bevan (4) and John (23), although his name will always be linked with Barry John. Their partnership was intuitive, and the pair always communicated in Welsh. Like John, albeit not quite as drastically prematurely, Edwards got out at a time when he could easily have played on. His competitive spirit was never more in evidence than when he scored that fabulous try against Scotland in 1972, breaking from his own half, kicking on, and winning the race for a touchdown that left him covered in mud. Spike Milligan said afterwards that they should have commemorated the moment by building a cathedral on the spot. It was at the opposite end of the same ground that he scored an even more famous try for the Barbarians against Ian Kirkpatrick's 1972/73 All Blacks when Phil Bennett side-stepped from under his own posts and counter-attacked to give the home fans a rare live chance of seeing the magic of the 1971 British Lions. As commentator Cliff Morgan was heard to say on more than one occasion in the '70s: 'Oh, that man, Edwards!'

CHAPTER 14

BATTLE FOR
WORLD
SUPREMACY

IN THE ONGOING BATTLE against commercialism, the Rugby Football Union were beginning to resemble the battiest of all the English monarchs. Canute-like, they stood upon the shore, but while the waves had once prompted nothing more drastic than the occasional rolling up of a trouser leg, by the mid-1970s, they were in serious need of a snorkel and flippers. In the early years they had managed to contain the threat of professionalism by their own authoritarian rule, and a hanging's-too-good-for-them attitude that only just stopped short of throwing the book at anyone caught reading the rugby league results in the morning newspaper. Players spotted boarding a train heading any further north than Newport Pagnell would still need to have a damned good explanation, but the climate now was running inexorably against the self-appointed guardians of amateurism.

The success of the British Lions in the early '70s had a beneficial effect on international rugby in that it created argument, interest and discussion. Who was the best in the world?

The northern hemisphere, albeit in the guise of a combined side, could now take on and beat the best from the south, but in the absence of any specific competition involving the leading nations taking each on at the same time and on the same stage, the title of world champions would always carry the slightly unsatisfactory prefix of 'unofficial'.

New Zealand were still the side to beat, or for the rest to measure themselves against, given that South Africa had by now conceded that privilege by dictating that victory over them entitled a side to call themselves the best in the world just so long as the world was populated by white people only. Australia were also strong, and in the northern hemisphere, the 1970s was a decade in which every side staked out a claim at one time or another. Wales, with three Grand Slams in 1971, '76 and '78 were the dominant home nation overall, while England ended a twenty-three-year wait with a Grand Slam of their own in 1980.

Other international sides, however, were beginning to challenge the established order – Romania, Argentina, Fiji and Samoa. Argentinian fly half Hugo Porta had many supporters as the finest fly half in world rugby. Fiji had played their first overseas international against Western Samoa in Apia in 1924. The match started at 7 a.m. to allow the home players to get to work. Fiji won 6–0, despite the presence of a large tree on the halfway line. The Fijians played barefoot; the first time boots were worn was against the NZ Maoris at Suva in 1948, although most had been taken off and thrown away before the final whistle. Fiji lost 24–6. Boots were also a problem for Tonga. An old handbook includes the following statement: 'We prefer rugby to cricket. Rugby jerseys last four years. We can't afford cricket balls, they are too expensive. Boots are a problem. The RFU forced us to wear them in 1940.' Gibraltar has one pitch and that is grassless, so a form of touch rugby is played there, while rugby has been popular in Japan since the 1920s. Details of the game were published in *The Land of the Rising Scrum*. It was rather different in the People's

Republic where the game was banned because, as the Sports Council explained, 'a meeting of sullied bodies in physical contact cannot be approved. There is no place for these elements in our society.' Not all communist regimes thought alike, however, and the game received a great boost in Yugoslavia in 1964 when the authorities told all clubs to stop playing rugby league and change to the union code.

All these teams were either touring or hosting other international visitors, and with rugby beginning to enter the realms of big business, the clamour was growing for a properly organised and recognised competition between them all. Cricket had managed it in 1975, albeit only in its one-day format, and now people were wondering whether something similar would not be viable for rugby union.

The southern hemisphere nations were quick to recognise that this would be possible only if the players themselves were permitted to share in any financial success, and were already lobbying for players to be allowed to endorse products. 'Eat three Shredded Wheat for breakfast, and you too can look like Colin Meads.' However, it was entirely predictable for the RFU to be in the vanguard of opposition, viewing any such idea as entirely alien to the sacred code of amateurism. The twentieth century had been a consistent shock to the system for the RFU, what with devilish inventions like the horseless carriage and the telephone, and they saw it as nothing less than their moral duty to make sure that nothing divisive ever crept into the game – like change, for instance – unless, of course, it affected their own capacity for climbing into bed with a variety of sponsors.

In fairness to the RFU, they were merely the loudest voice in a northern hemisphere environment that viewed anything new with deep suspicion, and even when it became clear that the climate was ripe and a world championship inevitable, they had to be dragged to the table kicking and screaming. It was as though they'd been invited to dinner at Castle Dracula, and they weren't about to turn up without several cloves of garlic and a wooden stake secreted about their persons.

It was, therefore, left to the southern hemisphere to take the crucial initiative, which is why the first-ever Rugby World Cup – which could and should have been held at the original home of the game – was eventually staged, in an atmosphere of fudge and compromise, in New Zealand and Australia. And once installed in 1987, it took precisely one month of truly spectacular rugby to establish the World Cup as the blue riband event. The Lions, Tri-Nations and home internationals would all continue to have their own place in the overall scheme of things, but everything would now be secondary to the one truly global festival of rugby.

Australia's close involvement in that first-ever competition was both significant and well merited. The fact that they had managed to remain with rugby union's international élite – never mind beat them on several occasions – was almost as remarkable as anything the game had seen. Rugby union in Australia had always come a distant third behind rules football and league, and whenever Australia's amateur game gave birth to a star performer, he was – with one flourish of the chequebook – spirited away to another code.

The game in Australia began in New South Wales, who provided the official controlling body until the Australian Rugby Union was formed in 1949. The first official international was played in 1899 at the Sydney Cricket Ground against a British representative side, and one of their early legendary figures was H.H. 'Dally' Messenger, who played for the NSW side that beat the All Blacks in 1907. Like so many, Messenger turned professional, coming to Britain with the New Zealand rugby league side, and such was his kicking prowess that he was offered lucrative terms – including £2000 from Tottenham Hotspur – by several leading English soccer clubs. However, Messenger returned home with the missionary goal of establishing rugby league in his native country, and his success can be measured by the simple inscription underneath his portrait at the Australian Rugby League head-quarters, 'The Master'.

He received considerable assistance from union's knack of firing both barrels of the shotgun unerringly into its feet. When a popular player by the name of Alick Burden broke his shoulder in a match and had his claim for loss-of-earnings compensation turned down by the NSW Union, it was just the catalyst that was required for those in both Australia and New Zealand who had been agitating for a professional game. Rugby league made such rapid progress that union quickly found itself isolated as the minority code.

There was soon to be a nice little earner for the newly formed New Zealand rugby league team in the shape of three demonstration matches (under union laws) at the Sydney Showground, organised by the celebrated Australian cricketer, Victor Trumper. The tourists were guaranteed £750 for three matches, and the Australians, nicknamed the Pioneers, were given ten shillings per game plus expenses. The exception was Messenger, who, in the same way as English cricket clubs charged extra whenever W.G. Grace was playing, received £150 per match. Messenger's presence was regarded as essential to the growth of league in Australia, and the games also provided a boost to New Zealand's coffers when the short tour made them a profit of £200.

The year following Messenger's appearances in Britain with the New Zealand league side, the Australian rugby union team arrived in the UK, having set off with an argument over what they ought to call themselves. For some reason, given the fact that Australia was better known for marsupials, billabongs and convicts than small burrowing creatures, there was a strong faction within the NSW committee in favour of naming their team the Rabbits. However, after the players – not surprisingly – told them to hop off, they settled on the Wallabies.

In spite of this, their chosen mascot was a snake, one of Australia's rare non-venomous varieties, who went by the name of Bertie. Despite the fact that the majority of Australia's original settlers had been recommended for the trip by stern-faced men wearing wigs inside the Old Bailey, the UK Customs officials saw no reason to conduct any more thorough a search than normal, and Bertie made an illegal entrance into the country wrapped around the torso of one of the players. It was no great surprise when Bertie succumbed almost immediately to the British climate, although the loss of their mascot apparently had no detrimental effect on morale, given their 24–3 victory over Devon in the opening game.

It was on this tour that the Australians became Olympic champions. The Games were held in London in 1908, and the county champions, Cornwall, had been nominated to represent Britain. The tourists had already beaten them 18–5 when they met at the Olympic Stadium in Shepherd's Bush, and this time the scoreline was an even more emphatic 32–3 to the Wallabies. Australia suffered a narrow defeat, 9–6, at the hands of Wales, but hit back after conceding an early try against an England side containing ten new caps to win with three tries of their own. However, while it was a relatively successful tour in terms of results on the field, the raising of the players' profile created an increasingly familiar scenario off it. Thirteen members of that side switched to league after accepting offers of £100 per man, and it was a long time before the union team recovered.

There was one occasion when the Australians changed from calling themselves the Wallabies. On the 1927/28 tour to the British Isles they appeared as the Waratahs. This was because one of the only two states to make up the Australian Rugby Union, Queensland, had temporarily withdrawn their membership, leaving New South Wales to provide the representation. In the circumstances, three wins and two defeats in the five Tests was a pretty good achievement. The Waratahs were led by A.C. Wallace, one of the famous Scotland threequarter line in the side that had completed the Grand Slam in 1925. The tourists beat Wales, Ireland and France, but lost to Scotland and England, the latter awarding full caps in what they regarded as a full international.

It was the All Blacks who traditionally brought the best out of the Australians, and in 1929 New Zealand lost all three Test matches during their tour there. This was the first time that Australia had been able to field a fully representational side since 1914, and the series was marked by a cap for Gordon Sturtridge of Victoria, the first player outside NSW or Queensland to be selected. The origin of the Bledisloe Cup series between the two nations dates back to 1932 (the All Blacks won 2–1) and a trophy donated by the Governor-General of New Zealand, Lord Bledisloe. Some of the gloss was missing from that first encounter, given that his Lordship proffered his regrets for non-attendance, citing, in the true spirit of the amateur game, work commitments. It's doubtful whether his presence was greatly missed or mourned, although it would have been nice had the trophy itself been available to the winning team. It was still at the silversmiths when the All Blacks won, and it must have been hard to puff themselves up with pride when whoever was standing in for his Lordship said something along the lines of, 'Well done, boys. The trophy's in the post.'

The Wallabies again performed with credit in South Africa in 1933, going down by a narrow 3–2 margin, and by this time one or two characters were starting to emerge. The Springboks, by all accounts, were not short of competition in the roughing-up department, notably from the Australian forward W.H. 'Wild Bill' Cerutti, who had made the switch to rugby from soccer because there were not enough punch-ups for his liking in the latter. In 1934 Australia won the Bledisloe Cup for the first time, an achievement made all the more memorable by the fact that this time the trophy was available for presentation.

The Australians, with not very astute timing, arrived in Britain for a tour in 1939, so their greatest achievement (after leaving without playing a match) was to complete the voyage home again without being torpedoed. When they returned in 1947/48, the only survivor from that prewar selection was

Bill McLean, and he promptly broke a leg. This was the tour on which the Wallabies ran out of money for their return trip – via the USA and Canada for exhibition games – and were rescued by funds generated from the first Barbarians–tourists match. Their next tour to Britain in 1957/58 is best remembered for the game against England at Twickenham, when an injury to Phil Horrocks-Taylor forced flanker Peter Robbins to move into the centre, and the home team to play for fifty minutes with fourteen men. England, however, prevailed, thanks to one of the most celebrated tries in the game's history from Peter Jackson. The Australians, in that earthy way of theirs, were later to name a cigarette after him.

The Welsh game marked one of Carwyn James's two caps, and his only one in his club position of fly half, after Cliff Morgan withdrew through injury. Wales won 9–3 and, close though it was, it was still the biggest margin between Australia and any of the home nations during the four Tests. England and Ireland both won 9–6, and Scotland 12–8, it was the first time a touring team had failed to win a single international in Britain.

By the 1960s the Australians had an altogether more powerful side, and in 1963 they drew a series against the South Africans. In 1966 Ken Catchpole and Phil Hawthorne inspired them to a famous victory over Wales in Cardiff. It spoiled the debuts of Barry John and Gerald Davies, and marked the Wallabies first-ever win over the Welsh. In beating England on that same tour, they took the record for the most points – 23 – scored by a visiting side at Twickenham since the stadium opened in 1910, with Hawthorne becoming only the second player – after Pierre Albaladejo of France – to drop three goals in a Test. However, the tour ended in disappointment with defeats at the hands of Ireland, Scotland and France, coupled with the loss of Hawthorne immediately afterwards, lured away by an offer of 30,000 Australian dollars from the St George's Rugby League club.

Shortly after that, the Wallabies met the All Blacks at Sydney in one of the first internationals to allow injury replacements and, although it was some consolation at the time to have John Hipwell come on for Catchpole, the Australian scrum half was so badly damaged by Colin Meads yanking him out of a ruck that he was never to play again. The loss of Hawthorne and Catchpole in such a short period was a grievous blow to Australian rugby, but it soon gave warning of its growing ambition by turning out a series of stunningly talented schoolboy sides, several of which toured the UK. And in 1984, six years after the All Blacks had achieved their first-ever Grand Slam against the home nations, the Wallabies matched it with Alan Jones as coach and Andrew Slack as captain. They had quality players in the backs with Roger Gould, David Campese, Mark Ella, Michael Lynagh and Nick Farr-Jones, and were not short of hard, abrasive men up front.

If rules football, a game which appeared to have very few rules at all, was the natural home for very large Australians with a predilection for violence, rugby union was not all that far behind, as England had discovered on their tour down under in 1975. They suspected that the Australians might not have been of the prisoner-taking variety when they learned who was coaching them – a gentleman by the name of David Brockhoff, who had gained a certain notoriety as a player after the Second World War. During the 1949 Australian tour to New Zealand, Brockhoff's reputation was such that, even before the start of the game against West Coast/Buller, the referee felt obliged to knock on the visitors' dressing room door and issue him with a warning. Brockhoff listened intently, nodded in polite acquiescence, then ran out and launched himself so violently at the opposition that he was removed from the field. Brockhoff's pre-match team talks were less of a last-minute reminder about tactical considerations as an invitation to fix bayonets, and there were so many punch-ups that the Test matches required an MC rather than a referee. The English forwards did not take the Australian intimidation lying down – well, not metaphorically at any rate – and the ball often became something of an irrelevance. There were times, too, when it became invisible.

Physical though they were, the Australians were also great innovators, and came up with a tactic known as the up-your-jumper move. This had nothing to do with lifting in the line-out, but was a ploy designed to confuse the opposition. Upon the award of a penalty, the Australians would turn their backs on England and shove both hands up their jumpers, so that when they turned around again, no one knew who had the ball. It was outlawed almost immediately, but was amusing to watch at the time.

The 1984 Wallabies had the customary mixture of brain and brawn, and their skill and organisation were too much for the home countries. However, by way of illustration that touring sides were by now focusing almost entirely on the Test matches, Australia's Grand Slam side actually lost four games on that trip – to Cardiff, Ulster, Llanelli and the South of Scotland. The 19–3 victory over an England side fielding six new caps could have been more emphatic had Lynagh not left his kicking boots back in the dressing room, and Wales and Scotland were also comparative pushovers. Only the Irish proved awkward. The Scotland game was memorable for a brilliant try from Campese, who was establishing himself as one of the game's truly devastating running threequarters, and Campese also showed off his full range of talents in the Barbarians game. However, despite the Australians entering into the spirit of this end of tour showpiece, there was a growing feeling that the Baa-Baas match had become, for most tourists, a slightly irritating and irrelevant postscript at the end of an arduous tour.

It was certainly an anachronism, but an enjoyable one, in a rugby world now geared solely to winning as opposed to entertaining. The first World Cup in 1987 gave spectators the best of both worlds. There was no game – particularly when it got down to the serious business at the quarter-final stage – that could remotely be described as a friendly, but as a spectacle it was unsurpassed.

This first World Cup would take place without South Africa, by now more isolated than ever in their all-white laager. Rugby, with its almost masonic ideal of friendship, had been a good deal slower than other sports to desert them, but finally kicked them into touch. Even the New Zealanders, for whom rugby was never more important than it was in a series against the Springboks, were split, as was demonstrated – literally – in 1981. The disturbances were every bit as fierce as those during the Springbok tour of the UK in 1969/70, with rival factions actually brawling in the high streets, and when demonstrators swarmed on to the pitch before the tourists' second match against Waikato, the game was abandoned. They didn't even get that far with the South Canterbury fixture, the match being called off beforehand at the request of the local forces of law and order.

The Springboks had been forced to train 400 miles away from the venue for the first Test in Christchurch, and spent the night before the game in makeshift beds in a local rugby club. They drove to Lancaster Park a full five and a half hours before the scheduled kick-off, which was then delayed as tin-tacks, fish hooks and broken glass were removed from the playing surface. South Africa, having won all their provincial games, went into the final Test level at 1–1 in the three-match series. It was a match that was to become famous for an aerial bombardment, not in the rugby sense, with full backs cowering underneath garryowens, but for yet another form of political demonstration. Leaflets and flour bombs rained down on the pitch, dropped by a protesting aviator. One of these bombs hit an All Black, Gary Knight, which at least left him a colour acceptable to the opposition.

> *From what I could see, it was our players who were to blame for starting the punch-ups . . . When you're losing and feeling inferior, you sometimes lose control.*
>
> DANIE CRAVEN, South African RFU president, after Springboks Test defeat at Christchurch, 1981

After clearing up the booby traps in the grass, there was another delay at the kick-off when a bogus referee pinched the ball and kicked it into the crowd, prompting the real ref – Clive Norling of Wales – to secure the agreement of both sides to make up any time lost through demonstrations. It was the first-ever case of injury time being added on for a man being hit by a flour bomb, but it was to win the All Blacks the series. Long after the official eighty minutes were up, and with the sides level, New Zealand finished the Springboks off with a long-range Allan Hewson penalty.

By the time 1987 came around, there was no prospect at all of South Africa getting an invitation to the party, with the major remaining countries being joined by the USA, Fiji, Japan, Italy, Argentina, Tonga, Romania and Zimbabwe. And it was Fiji who joined the big seven – England, Scotland, Ireland, Wales, New Zealand, Australia and France – in the quarter-finals. Wales's reward for beating England at that stage was to qualify for ritual humiliation (49–6) at the hands of the All Blacks in the semi-final, which at least prepared the Welsh for the worst on their trip to New Zealand the following year, when they lost 52–3 and 54–9. The other semi-final was between Australia and France, with the French – through Serge Blanco's last-minute try – spoiling a final that had been scripted beforehand as a private dust-up between the host countries. New Zealand won the final comfortably, still without their official captain Andy Dalton who had been injured throughout the tournament. Sean Fitzpatrick played all six matches, but it was scrum half David Kirk who became the first man to get his hands on the new trophy.

The experience of two countries staging the tournament had caused a number of logistical problems, and one of the first recommendations from the organisers was that the next World Cup, in 1991, should go to just a single country. It came as no surprise to students of rugby history, therefore, when the next tournament actually went to five countries – the home nations and France. Two different sets of broadcasters was just one of a number of difficulties and, after Scotland had refused to allow Twickenham to handle the overall marketing with a guaranteed sum, the tournament wobbled from one commercial cock-up to another. The 1987 World Cup had really marked the countdown to the end of rugby union's amateur days, and by 1991 it was a money-driven major event. However, when it finally came around, and rugby's amateur leaders dipped their first elbow into the bathwater of big business, they lost several layers of scalded skin in the process.

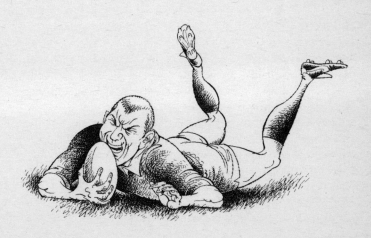

CHAPTER 15

THE BREAKING
WIND OF CHANGE

I<small>T WAS, THE</small> RFU <small>AGREED</small>, a terrible business. The biggest crisis the game had seen since the great split of the nineteenth century. The advent of the World Cup made it clear that the unthinkable had happened. After a hundred odd years of running English rugby with all the vision, enlightenment and generosity of a Victorian parent, this was how they were going to be repaid. There was no shortage of people clamouring for a voice in how the game was now being structured and organised and, heaven knows, a benevolent body like the RFU was more than prepared to lend a sympathetic ear. But the players? My God. No one was really advocating a return to the days of the old Empire, when native insurrection was put down with a ruthless slap on the colonial wrist, but this was almost a case for sending in the gunboats.

England, as had been the case a century earlier, were at the epicentre of all discussions, moves and pressures to surrender to the commercial interests of the game, and the players, who had previously been invited to remember the old parental doctrine which involved little boys being seen but not heard, were now the most unruly element in the entire classroom. The cake – thanks to the huge impact of the World

Cup – was out of the oven, and the players wanted a slice of it.

This was thrown into even sharper focus for the RFU by the fact that England were enjoying great success on the field, via an ungrateful generation of players no longer content to accept the crumbs and platitudes from the committee room table. They could not have inspired the climate for change on their own, but with the relaxing of some of the stricter clauses of amateurism in New Zealand and Australia, and the obvious commercial opportunities thrown up by the World Cup, the England players were threatening to be the first pebble in an inevitable avalanche.

One person above all, William David Charles Carling, was starting to epitomise the mood among rugby players all over the world. They wanted an end to their traditional serfdom, and they wanted a hand in the way the game was now being run – not to mention having an authorised hand in the till. Carling was to acquire a profile way, way above the average international rugby player, and was also to become responsible for an expression which very quickly transcended its original rugby context and became symbolic of the generation gap right across the spectrum – 'Old Fartism'.

Will Carling was not rugby's first superstar, nowhere near, in fact. He wasn't even England's. That title belonged to Wavell Wakefield who, like Carling, was a product of Sedbergh School. Colin Meads was the last of the old-style greats, while there were a number of contenders – such as Gareth Edwards – for the title of rugby's first modern icon. Latterly, the likes of Michael Jones, Serge Blanco, Jonathan Davies, Jeremy Guscott, Gavin Hastings and David Campese strode the world stage, and yet it was Carling who became the symbol of the modern rugby player, on and off the field, mainly because of his position as England's rugby captain.

Carling had been appointed captain of his country at the age of twenty-two and, unusually, held on to the job for the next eight years. The captaincy gave the media licence to turn the spotlight on a young, ruggedly good-looking sportsman who wore designer clothes, drove flash cars, and had a private life that was, to put it mildly, interesting. To the RFU, of course, Carling was as much a symbol of rebellious youth as the teddy boy, with his drainpipe trousers, Brylcreemed quiff and beetle-crusher shoes, had been in the 1950s. The RFU tried to bring him down, but failed, and it was Carling's private life – a contradiction in terms if ever there was one – which ultimately did for him. Rugby union's impending divorce from amateurism was played out in nothing like the intense spotlight of Carling's own divorce.

The backcloth to all this was the long history of underachievement in English rugby, as was the case in many other sports that England invented, nurtured and exported. Innate conservatism made this more or less inevitable, and the spirit of experiment was left to others. England's administrators were consumed by negative thoughts rather than positive ones, and whenever the time seemed ripe to step into the laboratory, they did not so much conjure up images of Dr Pasteur as Dr Jekyll.

The same applied to soccer, which was hijacked by the rest of the world, leaving England, except for one memorable occassion in 1966, to wander on and off the stage as a bit-part player. There have been signs of willingness to change more recently, and there is now more money in English soccer than almost anywhere else, but while other nations evolved and progressed, England never quite shrugged off their penchant for the old-style centre-half, who walked around with the imprint of a lace on a concave forehead. Cricket, too, lived in a leafy suburb of St John's Wood known as Memory Lane, immersed in a culture that placed imagery above substance, and a domestic structure run by anti-reformation old school ties and their various, flatulent committees. Graham Gooch, part of an era which spawned such talents as Gower, Botham and Willis, once likened the captaincy of England – in terms of the go-ahead attitude of its ruling body – as the equivalent of 'farting against thunder'.

Serge Blanco

The farts themselves, of course, suspected thunder in the clearest of blue skies, and when the custodians of rugby union got behind the wheel of the game, their initial instinct was to reach for the gear lever and select reverse. In a way the success of their sides in the 1920s and again in the 1950s could be put down to the exuberance of a generation glad not to be going off to war. After the success of Eric Evans' side in 1957, England were not to achieve another Grand Slam until Bill Beaumont's team did it in 1980.

It was in the '60s that English rugby truly lost its way. While the rest of the country was entering into the spirit of the so-called Swinging Sixties, the RFU looked through its monocle at an irrepressible younger generation and doubtless arrived at the conclusion that the hula hoop was some kind of Marxist plot. The air was thick with a new spirit of freedom, but when RFU officials spotted a cloud or two of it drifting towards Twickenham, they immediately broke out the gas masks.

It took Wales to light the touch paper of revolution. The RFU took a look at their success, noted that they were indulging in such things as appointing full-time coaching organisers, and decided that they had better have one of their own. However, the appointment of Don Rutherford in 1970 as RFU technical administrator was more of a sop than a bold leap into the future, and – with a transparent lack of dynamism – Rutherford held this post for more than a quarter of a century.

England, to no one's great surprise, continued to find it hard going on the field, and with the Welsh lording it over them time and again, England did not win in Cardiff between 1963 and 1991. And even when they ended that desperate sequence they managed – of which more later – to turn it into a public relations disaster.

They had their good moments, with John Pullin's side winning in South Africa in 1972 and a year later beating the All Blacks in Auckland, but mostly – and especially at home –

177

it was a sad old story of messy selection and dubious morale. The great shame of all this was that England invariably had as much individual talent at their disposal as any of the other home nations. In the 1970s, England had forwards who were more than a match for the Welsh in Fran Cotton, Mike Burton, Peter Wheeler, Pullin, Nigel Horton, Chris Ralston, Bill Beaumont, Roger Uttley, Andy Ripley, Peter Dixon and Tony Neary. There was talent in the backs as well, with Jan Webster, Steve Smith, Alan Old, John Finlan and David Duckham. As collective units, though, they only infrequently shone, and while there was obviously pride attached to wearing the white shirt, it was not as obvious as it was with those wearing red, green or blue. The RFU's idea of the thrill that ought to be associated with winning your first international cap is best illustrated by what happened to Peter Wheeler. While players from other countries had theirs presented in some kind of emotional ceremony, the RFU put his in the post. He got home one evening, in the pouring rain, to find it lying on the doorstep, half in and half out of a soggy paper bag.

Around this time, the very structure of the RFU – as was the case with the Test and County Cricket Board – actively worked against the creation of a successful national side. The major domestic competition was the hopelessly uncompetitive county championship, and yet the RFU committee charged with looking for better alternatives was made up entirely of county representatives. It was the turkeys voting for Christmas syndrome. Merit tables were given an outing, and in 1973 they came up with a club cup competition. The RFU Knock-out Cup was later sponsored by John Player, Pilkington and Tetley's Bitter. But in the overall scheme of things, few rugby men of substance and style had the chance to influence events, given that they were not prepared to sit around on endless, rule-bound committees. That was left to those who were happy to keep their heads down and nod in all the right places. Added to all this was the firm RFU conviction that they were the people who mattered, as opposed to the IB. Thus, as the

RFU found itself on a collision course with professionalism, it was a bit like watching them plan for nuclear war with one of Field Marshal Haig's old textbooks.

Team selection was also a constant eyebrow-raiser. Two English regional sides had beaten the All Blacks in 1972/73 – the first time in sixty-seven years of trying that any English team other than the national side had beaten New Zealand – but nothing like as comprehensively as the North's victory over New Zealand at Otley in 1979. As Budge Rogers, the chairman of selectors and for a long time England's most capped player, prepared to leave the ground after the North's 21–9 victory, a fan came up and shoved the match programme under his nose. 'There's your team for Saturday,' he said, referring to the following weekend's international at Twickenham. As it happened, Rogers and his co-selectors would have been forced to find a different full back from the Irishman Kevin O'Brien, but the other fourteen all qualified. There were five England captains in the pack – Cotton, Uttley, Neary, Dixon and Beaumont – and Steve Smith and Alan Old at half back. Old, in fact, was heavily fancied for the Lions No. 10 shirt in 1974 before being forced to fly home injured.

> *Never mind, you had the nicest jerseys.*
> WELSH SUPPORTER to chairman of England selectors after
> Wales's 27–3 win, 1979

However, if the All Blacks were worried about Twickenham, they perked up a bit when they saw the England team. Instead of Old, the selectors opted to give a debut to a running fly half in Les Cusworth, and Uttley and Dixon were discarded from the back row in favour of John Scott and Mike Rafter. It was as though Rogers had never made the trip to Otley, and although England lost by a single point, it still went down as a golden chance missed rather than a glorious failure.

The RFU, to their credit, may well have recognised that themselves, and were more on the right wavelength when they then appointed Mike Davis, straight from the England Schools set-up, as national coach. It was a bit of a shock, as Davis was known to be more of a players' man than one from the establishment, and he was later 'professionalised' by the same people who appointed him for the heinous crime of writing a book. It was never published, but – can you believe it? – merely the wicked intent was enough to nail him.

Davis should, so to speak, have taken a leaf out Andy Haden's book. When the All Black forward found himself on the carpet for writing his autobiography *Boots & All*, Haden, who rather enjoyed flouting the regulations, stated that, as he was a full-time author at the time of writing it, he had not broken any rules. Haden was a pretty good actor – as he showed when hurling himself out of the line-out against Wales in 1978 – and he got away with it. Haden's dive in that game preceded the All Blacks' last-minute winning penalty, although the referee claimed he had awarded it for a barge on Frank Oliver. The number of people who believed that could comfortably have been accommodated inside the same telephone box.

However, if Davis was not as streetwise as Haden in circum-navigating regulations, he did make his impact as a coach by steering England to that 1980 Grand Slam. Many players in that England side were approaching the end of their careers, and Davis balanced his team with a sprinkling of newcomers. In the pack he added the renowned scrummager Phil Blakeway and the giant lock Maurice Colclough; at half back, the steady, if un-electric pairing of Steve Smith and John Horton; and on the back of injuries to Nick Preston and Tony Bond, Davis went for the Leicester partnership of Paul Dodge and Clive Woodward in the centre.

After victory over Ireland in the opening game, the championship was set up with a thrilling win in Paris, scene of some fearful hammerings in the '70s. The Grand Slam was won at Murrayfield with a Woodward-inspired exhibition among the backs, although they very nearly made a mess of it all in the third match against Wales at Twickenham. The atmosphere before this game was not so much intense as evil, with both sides whipping things up in the newspapers, and a TV documentary having singled out Paul Ringer as a one-man hit squad. The Llanelli flanker had failed to endear himself to Leicester during a spell at Welford Road, and indeed to Saturday night pub diners with a party piece, during coach trips home, that occasionally involved dipping into the tropical aquaria that were popular at the time, and treating himself to a fish supper, washed down with a pint or two of ale.

Wheeler, who had played alongside him at Leicester, recalled later that the early exchanges at Twickenham had been so unsavoury that he feared the worst when he found himself trapped on the floor and saw a pair of chunky, red-stockinged legs trundling towards him. 'Then I saw who it was,' said Wheeler (he and the Welsh prop Graham Price had become firm friends on a Lions' tour), 'and thought, "Thank God for that, it's my old mate, Pricey." Then I saw the look in his eyes, and that was it. Crunch.'

England were not slow to put it about as it were, but it was Ringer who was next to offend after a final warning to both sides from Irish referee David Burnett, clattering late into fly half Horton. Ringer became the first player sent off at Twickenham since Cyril Brownlie in 1925, and although Wales – reduced to fourteen men after only a quarter of an hour – scored two tries to nil, it was Dusty Hare who won it for England with an angled penalty in the closing minutes.

Bill Beaumont had become the first England skipper to complete a Grand Slam since Eric Evans in 1957 and his reward was to become the first Englishman to lead the British Lions for fifty years. Beaumont might have struggled to survive in these days of lock forward giants, but he was an honest toiler in the second row who led the way, and he was a considerate soul off the field. His introduction to the rigours of international rugby and the ways of the England set-up came on the tour of Australia in 1975. Beaumont was already off the field receiving stitches in the dressing room when Mike Burton entered after becoming the first England international to be sent off. Beaumont thought he had better get back on the park and rushed to the touchline, where he was met by the England manager Alec Lewis and the memorable rhetorical question: 'Have you ever played prop before or will the next seventy-five minutes be your first attempt?'

Bill Beaumont

> *It was like MASH in the medical room.*
> LEON WALKDEN, RFU doctor, after violent England v Wales
> match, 1980

The 1980 Grand Slam, though, was a kind of rogue meteor in an era of under-achievement, and disappointment followed for the rest of the decade. The biggest blow was defeat by Wales in the 1987 World Cup quarter-final, which cost the then coach, Martin Green, his job. It was a symbolic gesture that went as far towards the root of the problem as moving a couple of deckchairs on the *Titanic*. Chairman of selectors Mike Weston wanted sole authority, but the RFU declined his thoughtful offer, and installed Geoff Cooke as coach. Cooke preached stability, but then got through five captains in less than a year. Finally, on the Saturday night a week before the 1988 Test against Australia, Carling was unveiled – two months before his twenty-third birthday – as the youngest England captain for fifty-seven-years and the tenth since Beaumont.

Carling was not the best centre England ever had, nor the greatest leader, but he did represent the face of English rugby in a way no one had ever seen before. The RFU had good reason to be grateful to Carling's England, in that it gave the whole of English rugby the largely illusory image of efficiency, organisation and teamwork. Yet the RFU spent most of those years attempting to take a chunk out of the hand that fed them. As far as they were concerned, they had the same feelings of affection for Carling as the Chicago Police Department had for Al Capone.

The Carling era began in emotional fashion with victory over multi-talented Australia, although Carling's slightly bemused expression afterwards had less to do with stunned elation as being carried off with concussion shortly before the end of the game. The Sunday newspaper headlines were ecstatic in their praise, not only for the victory, but the enterprising manner of it, and Carling became an overnight darling. England still managed to lose in Cardiff, though, and with injury keeping Carling out of the 1989 Lions tour, a young up and comer by the name of Jeremy Guscott took his place for the trip to Australia. In 1990 the final game of the season provided the first-ever instance of a Grand Slam, Triple Crown, Championship and Calcutta Cup all being on the line at the same time for both teams, and when England were beaten by the Scots, doubts about Carling's leadership began to surface.

However, back-to-back Grand Slams and a journey to the World Cup final in the next two seasons elevated Carling's status to a new level, and were the RFU delighted? Were they hell. They didn't care at all for this superstar malarkey, neither did they enjoy the fact that – largely on the back of Carling's own personal glamour – all the players were gaining expansive profiles. The RFU spotted the glimmer of a chance to bring him to heel soon afterwards when they got wind of Carling receiving a fee for opening a leisure facility near Croydon. 'And what did you do with this money, Mr Carling?' they asked, as he was hauled up before the beak. 'I gave it to charity,' said Carling. 'Er, ah, yes, well,' they spluttered, before going on to state that if Carling had sent the fee through them, rather than directly to the charity, it would have, ahem, saved him the tax. And, presumably, the inquisition.

Dudley Wood, the RFU secretary, was one of the most able administrators in the game, an ideal man to smooth the transition to professionalism in the 1990s, but as a fervent guardian of the old amateur code, he remained ideologically stuck in the 1890s. The sport's complex investigation was the second time Carling had been on the RFU's disciplinary carpet, following a demand for proof that he had not been paid for a modelling feature in *You* magazine. Carling, not unnaturally, rather resented the fact that, on both occasions, he had

Gavin Hastings

been guilty by implication until he could demonstrate otherwise. Carling was back in the news after offering some mild criticism of the footballer Paul Gascoigne at a Sports Forum evening, and was by now starting to envy people in slightly lower-profile jobs – the Prime Minister, for instance.

Victory in Cardiff for the first time in twenty-eight years should have taken some of the sting out of it, but the players celebrated this momentous event by declining to give a single interview. It was the result of the players themselves having set up a company to look after their own commercial interests, and having decided that it was all very well blubbing into microphones in their hour of triumph, and explaining just how it felt to plunge over for that match-winning try, but that this sort of thing was now a matter for a chap and his wallet rather than a team and its country. It was almost QED for the RFU. The name given to this company, by the way, was Player Vision, which, if nothing else, produced a laugh.

Predictably enough, however, the RFU produced an even bigger laugh when they pulled a Timberland advertisement from an England–Scotland match programme, in which several players were pictured wearing, 'Timberland' gear. The new amateur code allowed only non-rugby-related spin-offs, and Dudley Wood concluded that 'appearing in a rugby programme is clearly rugby related'. Had Timberland placed the advertisement outside Twickenham Tube station which is, after all, occasionally used by non-rugby-related commuters, it would presumably have been perfectly acceptable.

Back on the field, England had to get through two difficult away games to reach the final of the World Cup, firstly against the French in Paris, and then against Scotland at Murrayfield. The French lost a few admirers as well as the match when their coach, Daniel Dubroca, assaulted the New Zealand referee David Bishop in the tunnel, and the Scots clearly harboured no ill feelings when they lost, judging by the way Gavin Hastings and his team turned up for the final wearing Australian scarves. England, heavily criticised throughout the tournament for their one-dimensional rugby, surprised the entire country by flinging the ball around against Australia, and Carling – one of the architects of the change of plan – was not very popular with his forwards for what they saw as a tactical blunder.

Carling's popularity pendulum rarely hovered anywhere in the neutral zone, and after becoming *Rugby World* Player of the Year in 1992, he was overlooked for the Lions captaincy in 1993 in favour of Hastings. Three days after Hastings was appointed, Carling announced his engagement to Julia Smith, and such was his media status, it made the front pages.

He made them again in 1995, shortly before England headed off to South Africa for the World Cup. Carling had been filmed for a Channel Four documentary, after which he made what he thought – or so he said – was an off-camera, off-the-cuff remark concerning the RFU committee. He referred to them, with admirable generosity some might say, as 'fifty-seven old farts'. Channel Four clearly didn't share Carling's view that this had not been intended for public consumption, as they used the clip to promote the programme. It might have remained a verbal molehill but for the RFU president, Dennis Easby, going some considerable way towards proving Carling's point by an outburst of pomposity that transcended even the RFU's generous guidelines. He has gone too far this time, spluttered Easby at the Norwich Rugby Dinner, using the platform to extol the virtues of the unsung, hard-working stalwarts at HQ.

Ten days before the team was due to leave for South Africa, and on the morning of the Pilkington Cup final, the Rugby Union issued the following statement. 'It has been decided with regret that Will Carling's captaincy of the team will be terminated forthwith, and an announcement concerning his replacement will be made shortly. In the light of the view Will Carling has expressed regarding administrators, it is considered inappropriate for him to continue to represent England as captain, the Rugby Football Union, England, and indeed English sport.' Consider the breathtaking fartishness of those last few words.

The RFU were so far divorced from the real world that the public could not believe it. Neither could the England players, who quickly made it known that they could appoint who they liked. No one would take the captaincy. Under pressure, the RFU announced that they had actually been lenient by not removing Carling from the World Cup squad itself, but it was by now clear that their position was untenable. In the circumstances, it was quite a gesture for Carling's agent, Jon Holmes, to broker a peace deal in which the captain was reinstated in return for an apparent climbdown. The moment was marked by pictures of Carling and Easby shaking hands, and there was little doubt in the public mind about which one of them represented the jackass. At least Easby deserved some sympathy for fronting up. One or two others with blood on the knife were keeping their heads well below the parapet.

England's World Cup challenge was spiked in the semi-final by a charging rhinoceros wearing an All Black No. 11 jersey, but Jonah Lomu was soon a distant memory for Carling, who by now was having to look at the society pages to find out what was being written about him. The *News of the World* had casually mentioned – over about twelve pages – that his relationship with the Princess of Wales was based on rather more than a mutual interest in threequarter play, and when it was revealed that Carling had been back to Kensington House after the story had appeared, his marriage was on the road to breaking up.

His personal life went from bad to worse in the public glare and led to the collapse of Carling's benefit season – including a special match planned for Wembley – and also contributed to the break-up of several friendships. As plots go, it would have been a bit far-fetched even for Jeffrey Archer, but it certainly raised rugby's profile at a time when it was just about to take the plunge into full-time professionalism.

In March 1996, a mile or two down the road from

Twickenham on the very morning England won the championship, a man woke up in a Putney hospital after spending seven years in a coma. His first recorded words are not known, but it would not have been a huge surprise if they were something along the lines of: 'Bloody hell. Is Will Carling still England captain?'

And yes he was, albeit for the last time. Remarkably Carling had remained in the job from November 1988, with forty-four victories from fifty-nine matches. Under his leadership, England had also reached the 1991 World Cup final, the 1995 semi-final, had won the Grand Slam in 1991, '92 and '95, the Triple Crown and championship in '91, '92, '95 and '96. Furthermore, Twickenham had almost become the same unstormable citadel that Cardiff had been for Wales in the 1970s.

The England captaincy has been shared around since his stepping down in 1996. Phil de Glanville took over under Jack Rowell, but Lawrence Dallaglio was new coach Clive Woodward's choice when he was appointed in 1997. But Dallaglio went down in a blaze of front-page allegations of drug-taking that led to him being found guilty of bringing the game into disrepute. Martin Johnson, who had led the 1997 Lions, took over through to the World Cup, but injury kept him out of Six Nations 2000 and scrum half Matt Dawson took charge. Then a problem shoulder for Dawson meant that Johnson was back in charge for the 2000 tour to South Africa, where a shared series indicated Johnson will take some shifting.

CHAPTER 16

PAY UP, PAY UP, AND PAY THE GAME

INTERNATIONAL RUGBY PLAYERS had lived a hand-to-mouth existence trying to make a few bob on the side. Match tickets were a regular source of income, especially on tour when the money would be collected for the players' pool and generally spent on a party. The game got itself in a dreadful tizz during the early 1980s when it was revealed that adidas had been paying players 'boot' money. That, traditionally, was where it had been stuffed for over a century, but this new reward was for wearing adidas boots, or if not, for allowing the representative to paint three stripes down the side. The dazzling Welsh side of the '70s had attracted the attention, but top players from all countries were implicated. Such was the furore at the RFU, that one president suggested sending the England Under-19 team into the international championship to make sure none of the side was tainted. But it was small change. England fly half Huw Davies remembers sitting on the England replacements' bench and finding himself rather cramped for room. He wasn't too surprised to find a bescarfed fan sitting on the end, having been sold the space by one the England forward replacements!

In 1995 rugby made the final leap from the shrinking world of amateurism into full-blown professionalism and, as leaps go, it was every bit as astounding as the one made by Bob Beamon at the 1968 Olympics, when he almost cleared the long-jump pit, or Evel Knievel launching his motorbike over seventeen double-decker buses. Knievel ended up being extricated from a heap of twisted metal and loaded into the back of an ambulance, which is very nearly what happened to rugby as well.

In order to appreciate fully just what a chasm there was between the game that had been played for over a hundred years and this new model, it is fairly instructive to go back to the somewhat different world of the 1999 and 2000 Premiership champions Leicester, as it was in the 1980s when I was covering their progress as correspondent for the local evening newspaper.

The very first piece I wrote concerned the dropping of their fly half, Bleddyn Jones, which resulted – to my mild astonishment – in a series of apoplectic telephone calls from various committee men. 'Listen here, old chap,' was the gist of it. 'You can't describe someone as being "dropped" in rugby union. You should be saying that he is having a run-out for the Extra 1st XV.' This was news to Jones, of course, who had indeed considered himself dropped, but it was a good example of how rugby people – even at the top level – would bridle at the public being informed that rugby football was in any way related to something as grubbily professional as association football. 'It's a players' game' was the constant refrain, the inference being that it was really none of the media's business – unless, of course, they would be so kind as to let everyone know the time of Saturday's kick-off.

The other thing I quickly learnt was that the nastiest, dirtiest matches were those played between policemen or doctors or teams that lived locally. The Hospitals Cup finals and clashes between the British Police and the French Police were often X-rated, although participants included British Lions and internationals. Rugby never needed money for real needle and rivalry on the field – Oxford v Cambridge, England v Scotland, North v South, South Africa v New Zealand. And being international team-mates meant nothing. A prop and a hooker may have had their arms around each other the previous Saturday in the national cause, but six days later the sole object of this week's eighty minutes would be to inflict as much damage as possible on your opponent before buying him a pint in the bar and gloating about his injuries.

> *I prefer rugby to soccer . . . I enjoy the violence in rugby, except when they start biting each other's ears off.*
> ELIZABETH TAYLOR, film star, 1972

Needless to say, I was encouraged to preview a match in such a way that the spectators would be keen to see it, although this became a little difficult when key players started dropping out for reasons ranging from 'Can't get time off work' to 'He's away at a mate's wedding'. Can you imagine Leicester shaping up for a crucial match against Bath nowadays, and me having to write, 'Neil Back will miss this game as he is having his hair done, while Martin Johnson is also unavailable as his wife would very much like him to mow the lawn on Saturday afternoon.'

Away matches were always tense, if only for the fact that you were never quite certain of arriving anywhere with fifteen players. Dean Richards, for example, would be picked up from a roundabout near his home in Hinckley, while others gave vague instructions along the lines of: 'I'll be at Newport Pagnell services at about 1.30, just outside the gents.'

Then there were the tours. On the regular Easter trip to Wales, I once mounted a hotel staircase in Cardiff, and noted with satisfaction that Dusty Hare was clearly taking the game seriously as he was in bed very early. I was able to glean this from the fact that a bed was being propelled down the hotel stairs by several burly forwards, with Dusty, I noted as it whizzed past, still in it. His face was as white as one of the sheets. It was on this same trip that one of the props was sitting on the hotel wall on the Saturday morning while two of the backs filled a large plastic bag with bathwater, and hurled it out of a fifteenth-floor window. The explosion could be heard all round Cardiff as it hit the ground, and the prop got a drenching. Had it been a foot or two the other way, he would have come home in a hearse.

Every amateur club, big or small, had similar tales to tell, but at the highest level of the game, all that was to change. Ironically, some would say that nothing changed very much at all – squabbling over money, continuing southern hemisphere domination, the other home nations ganging up on England, personality clashes among the unions and, last but not least, the usual business about international player eligibility. It almost got to the point where the nation's forgers were tempted to chuck away their twenty-pound-note plates and start churning out birth certificates instead.

Professionalism had not officially arrived by the time of the 1995 World Cup in South Africa. The host nation were participating for the first time, following their own remarkable transition from a country in which the vast majority of the population were required to live out their lives in a metaphorical dog kennel, to a nation now governed by a black president. However, the tournament did bring to a head the spiralling conflict between commercialism and the old amateur values, and it was a huge success in bringing rugby to a wider audience – not least because of the emotional, high-profile presence of Nelson Mandela, who, had South Africa appeared in previous World Cups, would have been admitted only in order to clean the players' boots.

Despite their years of isolation, no one doubted that South Africa would be a major force on their own turf, and they began the tournament with victory – in front of Mandela – over the holders, Australia. This set up an England–Australia quarter-final, in which Rob Andrew's last-minute dropped goal reversed the result of the 1991 final at Twickenham. The general spirit of goodwill was not entirely apparent during the South Africa–Canada match, which resulted in three send-ings-off and two citings, although resulting suspensions did allow the coloured South African winger Chester Williams to be drafted in for the quarter-final against Western Samoa, in which he scored four tries.

South Africa then met France in a semi-final which was almost, and probably should have been, postponed because of a tropical downpour in Durban. The kick-off was delayed for an hour, and after an opening forty minutes more remi-niscent of a game of water polo than rugby, the Welsh referee Derek Bevan must have been seriously contemplating an aban-donment. He would probably have been lynched, as France would have gone through on a better disciplinary record, but South Africa finally splashed their way to victory.

In the other semi, England were demolished by New Zealand, who had earlier squeaked home narrowly against Japan by 145 points to 17 and, with Jonah Lomu leaving prostrate bodies in his wake whenever he got the ball, no one could really imagine them losing the final, not even to South Africa. However, it was to be decided in the Springboks' favour by sheer guts. The guts in their case meant their traditionally indomitable will to win, and the guts in New Zealand's case, so it was claimed afterwards, were those bits of intestine left behind in various hotel bathrooms after a bout of highly suspi-cious food-poisoning. Joel Stransky's dropped goal decided it, 15–12, but although the enduring image of the tournament is François Pienaar embracing Mandela, there are still those in New Zealand who feel that the Cup should have been presented to a South African chef rather than Pienaar.

The South Africans' big moment, however, was indelibly tarnished by a characteristically charmless performance from their own union president at the celebration dinner. Dr Louis Luyt was the man in overall charge of the World Cup. The arrogant Afrikaner autocrat announced, with no discernible trace of humour, that this had really been the first World Cup, as South Africa's exclusion had prevented them winning the first two. For the All Blacks, staring at both their food and Luyt with an equal amount of suspicion, it was like being invited round to dinner with the Borgias, and one of them, Mike Brewer, had to be physically restrained. Bevan, too, was humiliated by Luyt, who congratulated him for not abandoning the semi-final, and presented him with a watch by way of thanks. Bevan was left in tears.

Meantime, on 23 June, the day before the final, the southern hemisphere countries had announced a massive television deal with Rupert Murdoch, News Corporation stumping up US$550 million for the new Tri-Nations competition. Tony Hallett, who was to take over from Dudley Wood as RFU secretary a month later, understood perfectly well what was happening to the game. 'It appears obvious,' said Hallett, 'that however you dress it up, you will now have the full-time employment of guys to play rugby. To talk of funds going to the development of the game is just concealing the point. Perhaps they mean the development of the players' bank balances. It is no use talking about the death of amateurism any more. The term is already in a state of rigour mortis.'

Even if the priest was now at the bedside, however, most people (Hallett included most probably) at least expected amateurism to die a more lingering death. And no one expected the coroner to be called in at the IB's August 1995 meeting, at which a game involved in generations of fudge and compromise suddenly decided that it might as well go the whole hog. Ye gods. The first item of professional expenditure on the RFU balance sheet might well have been for a large consignment of smelling salts.

It is hard to say why the game took this single massive jump. The only irresistible pressure was for players to be allowed to exploit their own commercial status, a compromise which would certainly have been accepted in most quarters. However, the Establishment had probably prevaricated too long for it to stop there. Impatience had built up such a head of steam that the gasket simply blew off. And there may just have been an element of bloody-mindedness involved from the erstwhile champions of amateurism. 'You want it? Well, have the bloody lot then, and see where it gets you.' And chaos is what it threatened. Had, say, professionalism been confined to international rugby only, then the first-class game would have had more time to prepare for its own transition and given those involved enough scope to get their houses in order. It was one thing to open the floodgates, but quite another to pull the lever when there were so many around who couldn't swim.

True to form, it was the RFU who were slowest on the uptake. The biggest single priority now was to gain control of the leading players, but at Twickenham they were too worried about their bank overdraft to step in, and instead did what they did best – dithered. The leading players could comfortably have been bought up for around £50,000, which, together with additional club salaries and endorsements, could have taken an England international straight up to a six-figure remuneration. What happened instead was that the clubs led the financial revolution, with entrepreneurs stepping in to wave their chequebooks at anything in a pair of rugby shorts. The players were happy enough, but it left the clubs with wage bills that represented potential economic suicide. Not surprisingly either, the sudden transition led to internal squabbling and rancour. Hallett and the chairman of the RFU executive, Cliff Brittle, became embroiled in an unseemly power struggle and in April 1996 the RFU sprang a trick that surprised even Scotland, Wales, Ireland and France, who had not suspected that English arrogance could actually climb any higher.

When representatives of the other home unions picked up

their morning newspapers to learn that the RFU had negotiated its own personal TV deal (with Sky for £87.5 million) for the Five Nations, the outbreak of spluttering was so fierce that their kitchen walls were pebble dashed with cornflakes. Vernon Pugh, the Welsh chairman of the home unions' TV committee, exploded. 'This is selfishness gone mad,' he said. 'What infuriates us is that the deal has been done in a deceitful way.' And Pugh went on to warn what it all meant, namely, that the other countries would not play against England. Hallett claimed that the RFU's £35 million bank loan had forced them into going it alone, needing, as they did, as much money as possible in order to placate their leading clubs, who were threatening to break away. Scotland had been offered £20 million, Ireland £18 million, and Wales £40.5 million, which they rejected. Pugh said: 'We were offered twice as much as the others in an attempt to break us up, but there is no way we will abandon them, because to do that would be to abandon ourselves.' And privately, of course, the Welsh were in a rare old strop about England being offered more than the others put together.

The inevitable outcome was England being thrown out of the Five Nations, and the RFU countering with a 'Ya, boo, sucks' kind of response in which they announced that they would simply play more games against the southern hemisphere, and snootily insinuated that this would be better for them in the long run anyway. There were threats and counterthreats. No one seriously thought that home and away fixtures between Scotland and Ireland could make up for England's absence, or that a compromise would not ultimately be found. The other three home unions also knew that England could not survive on their own. Ultimately, England kept their deal, but without destroying the concept of money-sharing with regards to the Five Nations, as it then was. It appeared that the old pals act and the new professionalism were to have many more clashes.

Meantime, dyed in the wool Establishment figures took

themselves off to darkened rooms at the advent of the previously unthinkable notion of union and league coming together – both by players freely swapping between codes, and also in a two-leg exhibition between the different Cup winners, Bath and Wigan. Wigan won the league match 82–6 at Maine Road, and Bath the union game 44–9 at Twickenham. In between these two games, the blurring of codes increased when Wigan won the Middlesex Sevens.

By now all countries were at each other's throats as individuals became embroiled in power struggles, and such was the wrangle between Brittle and the club owners (not to mention between Brittle and his own executive) that he and John Hall, who had taken over at Newcastle, actually came to blows during a meeting. The club-union split in England got deadly serious in April of 1996 when the clubs (English Professional Rugby Union Clubs) threatened to quit all RFU competitions for the following season. They didn't, but it wasn't until May 1997 that a lasting truce was established when the clubs' demand for a twelve-team First Division was met.

The flood of money into club rugby began at Newcastle with Hall forking out a reputed £150,000 for Rob Andrew in September 1995, and in November, Saracens' benefactor, Nigel Wray, coughed up £2.5 million for Michael Lynagh, Philippe Sella and Kieran Bracken. Harlequins received a £1.5 million sponsorship deal from NEC, and the boxing promoter Frank Warren got involved at Bedford. The players, who had not long before been paying their clubs membership subs for the privilege of playing, and operating bar rotas to serve spectators after games, had seen the set-up alter so dramatically that the old concept of getting well-oiled after a match now applied to the hinges on their briefcases.

The 1997 victory for the British Lions in South Africa was a welcome diversion from all the political in-fighting, but a diversion is all it was. In July of 1997 a disastrous RFU AGM, in which its accounts were held up to ridicule, did for Hallett, who resigned as acting chief executive and headed off to Richmond. Less than two years later, Richmond went out of existence. Brittle was endorsed from the floor of the meeting, although a change in the executive failed to produce any change at all in the poisonous atmosphere. The English clubs even threatened to take the RFU to the European Commission over what they decreed to be illegal broadcasting and sponsorship procedures and in May of 1998 the next man to find his blood all over the boardroom carpet was Brittle himself.

In trying to establish a line between amateur and professional rugby, Brittle used the support of the junior clubs to keep him in power, but made a fatal tactical error when he tried to dismantle the sixty-two-man RFU council. It was the culmination of three years of bitter in-fighting, and it cost English rugby a small fortune. Had it not been for the Sir John Halls, and other millionaire owners, English rugby would have gone the same way as Wall Street in the 1930s with a long line of dole queues and soup kitchens.

Coinciding with Brittle's departure was the Mayfair Agreement announcing a peace treaty between the clubs and the union. The principle of release periods for international players was agreed, and appearances were limited to thirty-seven per player per season. The Premiership was increased from twelve to fourteen clubs, and the clubs agreed to play on international weekends. Extra demands at home, however, meant that there was less left for tough overseas missions on top, and after Clive Woodward became England's first-ever full-time professional coach in September 1997, he was left with something like a C team for England's tour to Australia the following summer – no Dallaglio, Johnson, Bracken, Catt, Rodber, Hill, Greenwood, Tony Underwood, Guscott, de Glanville or Grayson. Woodward put a brave face on it, hoping for a learning curve, and he was right in that at least. England learned how to lose heavily, and fly half Jonny Wilkinson, who had early that year become England's youngest Test debutant since 1927 aged eighteen years and 314 days, aged quite a bit in eighty minutes of utter humiliation. England were trounced 76–0 in Australia, and lost all their other matches on tour, including two Tests against New Zealand and one against South Africa.

The 1999 World Cup offered rugby the chance to present itself once again in a favourable light, not to mention expand its global horizons, but it failed lamentably thanks to poor organisation, scheduling, and the urge to give everyone a slice of the cake. It seemed to last forever, although up in Scotland, they didn't appear to be aware that there was a competition taking place at all. Increasing the number of teams to twenty did nothing but produce a series of hopeless mis-matches, and with their customary facility for over-complicating every-thing, the World Cup committee slotted everyone into five groups of four, instead of a more logical four groups of five. Most of the drama actually took place before the event, when there appeared to be every chance that Cardiff's new Millennium Stadium would not even be ready in time.

Wales, as hosts, had been exempt from qualifying, along with the holders, the 1995 finalists, and the third place winners. New Zealand and England (fourth in 1995) found themselves in the same group, and the traditional pipe-opener between hosts and holders was done away with because of the threat to Wales's progress from having South Africa in the same group.

The £125 million Millennium Stadium, on the site of the demolished National Stadium, did get finished, and an impres-sive structure it proved to be – which is more than can be said for the pitch. That turned out to be more suitable for a tribalistic Tuesday night dust-up between Abertillery and Ebbw Vale than for a showpiece game of international rugby. It was no small achievement to spend so much money on a state of the art stadium and yet produce a surface that appeared to be the product of a last-minute trip to the garden centre and a phone call to one of those 'no-job too small' ads in the *South Wales Evening Echo* classifieds. Retractable roof or not, it cut up horribly in the Wales–Australia quarter-final, when half an hour of drizzle was enough to turn parts of the playing surface into a bowl of chocolate blancmange.

Wales's own organisation also came in for critical scrutiny, with confusion at the ticket office, and the failure to schedule enough major matches in midweek giving the event the feeling of coming to a halt every weekend. The five-group format meant a play-off system, which certainly handicapped England because they had to play a hard game in midweek before their quarter-final in Paris. South Africa, the holders, were given the worst possible group in terms of focus and attention, while the TV pictures being beamed across the world from the games in Scotland mostly gave the impression of a ground having been vacated because of a bomb scare.

In the early stages the competition barely registered a pulse rate, never mind excitement, with England and New Zealand providing one of the few memorable games. England did well to recover from a 16–3 deficit before Lomu destroyed them again. The competition marked the retirement of Jeremy Guscott through injury during the group stage. Wales managed to finish top of their group, despite losing – as they had in 1991 – to the Samoans, but for all the pre-tournament hype about the northern hemisphere closing the gap, by the semi-finals it had turned into a virtual re-run of the Tri-Nations with South Africa, New Zealand, Australia – and France.

The competition was saved by two epic semi-finals, Australia overcoming South Africa in extra time with a Steve Larkham dropped goal, before France recorded an upset of astonishing proportions against a New Zealand side that had beaten them 54–7 in Wellington four months earlier. Despite the French ban on British beef, which sent all sorts of personal insults flying around in the popular press, Twickenham roared on the French in a game that prompted the veteran commentator Bill McLaren to remark: 'In four World Cup tournaments and some forty-two years of rugby coverage, I cannot recall a match of such enthralment, extraordinary physicality, and complete disregard of the odds.' France, having struggled to beat Fiji in a group game, quickly conceded two tries to Lomu, but then overwhelmed the All Blacks with a display of such off-the-cuff brilliance that they racked up 37 points without reply.

The fear for the final was that France had left all their rugby behind in this one game and so, sadly, it proved. The Wallabies' 35–12 victory was tediously one-sided, and the only real excitement was when the Queen (as she had in 1991) came to present the Cup to an Australian. On that same morning, Australia had gone to the polls over whether or not to retain the Queen as head of state, and it was no secret that the Australian captain John Eales, along with most of the squad, had voted by proxy for a republic a few weeks earlier at their country's High Commission. However, the fact that Australia as a whole had voted the other way round averted what could have been a slightly tricky presentation ceremony.

The first-ever Six Nations tournament will be remembered partly for Italy's winning debut, but mostly for arguments about players' family trees, and in Scotland, delight at depriving England of the Grand Slam that many people, both north and south of the border, felt they only had to turn up to collect. England had stuck by Woodward, despite the coach's constant requests when he took the job to be 'judged by the World Cup', and they looked in a class of their own when seeing off Ireland and Wales at home, and France and Italy in Paris and Rome. The Scots, by contrast, had provided the Italians with that historic victory, and were heading for a whitewash when England arrived for the final game at Murrayfield.

It could not have been a better afternoon for the Scots, who rampaged, harassed and intimidated in freezing rain and sleet, while England's tactics appeared to be based around a heat-wave and a bone hard pitch. If there was a Plan B, they kept it well hidden, and they left Murrayfield not only as losers, but bad losers to boot. Despite an official announcement that the Six Nations' Trophy, won by England the previous day when Wales beat Ireland, would be presented after the game, England left the pitch without collecting it. They claimed afterwards that they had not known about the planned presentation, neither would they have wanted to take the gloss of Scotland's victory by collecting it. Take the gloss off? Nothing would have delighted the Scots more than taunting the dejected English as they walked up for their consolation prize. And the English well knew it.

Scottish crowds take a traditional delight in questioning English parentage, but the entire question of ancestry was to dominate the championship, with Wales in particular being fingered so heavily that qualification appeared to be based around being able to produce an old theatre stub as proof of having attended Max Boyce's Christmas pantomime. And pantomime is about right, spawning jokes about Jonah Lomu being qualified for England on the grounds that his great-great grandfather ate Captain Cook. The first eyebrow-raiser concerned Brett Sinkinson, a New Zealander who had won fourteen Welsh caps by courtesy of a grandfather born in Carmarthen. Well, close-ish at any rate. Okay then, not too far away. Oldham, as it turned out. The spotlight then turned to the former All Black Shane Howarth, whose inclusion for Wales was justified on the basis that his Maori grandmother once had an affair with Thomas Williams, from Cardiff, and his mother was their illegitimate offspring. But there were no records of this; Howarth did have a connection with the old country – his grandfather on his father's side came from Romford in Essex. The issue had grown to such an exent by the time Howarth's replacement in the Welsh side, Matt Cardey, was selected to make his debut that Cardey had to wait until he'd proved that his grandmother had been born in the Gwent mining village of Nantyglo.

Then it was the Scots. David Hilton, forty-one caps, admitted that his 'qualifying' grandfather had actually been born in Bristol, and it was now becoming clear that there was no hard and fast procedure for examining such claims. The Australians were the most pious protestors, no doubt peeved by the way Wales poached – as they saw it – Jason Jones-Hughes. England, for the most part, kept clear of all the finger-pointing, having not selected any Russian princes (Obolensky) for some years. It certainly brought into focus qualification guidelines made of pure elastic, and sent people scurrying for the history books to find out who else had tenuous claims to wear certain coloured jerseys down the years. No one was sacred. One of the great Welsh heroes of the golden era, Gwyn Nicholls, who gave his name to a pair of gates at the Arms Park, was found to have been born in Westbury-on-Severn in Gloucestershire. There was also additional irony in the likes of Wales and Ireland being coached by New Zealanders in Graham Henry and Warren Gatland, and another All Black, Brad Johnstone – having coached Fiji in the World Cup – was now in charge of Italy. Furthermore, the 2001 Lions selected Henry as their coach after Scotland's Ian McGeechan, three times a Lions coach, pronounced himself unavailable for the trip to Australia. The All Blacks can now claim the series, whoever wins.

Money might be blamed for cutting an awful lot of family ties, and it is the chequebook rather than the birth certificate that continues to provide professional rugby with its more ticklish growing pains. But this controversy is not a product of the professional era. These qualifications did not come in until after the Second World War.

The European Cup, boycotted for a season by the English clubs, is currently the major club focus, and the latest plan – underwritten by a guarantee of £1.8 million per club – is for the top twelve to apply and pay for franchises from the 2001/02 season. The disappearance of Richmond, along with London Scottish, into the financial quicksand produced enough shock waves for a wage cap, although the clubs have already found a variety of side-steps to deal with that. Some of the entrepreneurs, such as Sir John Hall and Richmond's

Ashley Levett, have taken their bankrolls elsewhere, but others have remained true to their word of long-term investment. Most, if not all, of them may be perceived as carpet-bagging outsiders with no deep-seated love of the game, and yet who else put their hands up when the transition required bankrolling? Not the RFU, for sure.

At the time of writing, the professional game is off the teat, and long since on to solids, but is still having to be regularly burped to keep grizzling at bay, and toys from being hurled from the pram. There is no turning back, and not only would rugby have struggled to survive in its former incarnation, there is also no serious argument that it is a faster, fitter and higher-profile game than ever it was in the old amateur days. Whether it is a better game, however, remains a matter of opinion.

CHAPTER 17

NO SIDE

There was a time, and it seems long ago now, when an international rugby team's post-match celebration/sorrow-drowning would last a good deal longer than the actual preparation. When Colin Smart, whose surname was not quite appropriate to the deed, downed his bottle of aftershave in Paris, it passed into rugby folklore, Nowadays, your average prop forward would already have entered the after-game dinner with a dab of Gucci behind both ears, and far from a well-aimed bread roll in order to get the attention of the wine-waiter, he would only cause a fracas at the table if the orange juice was not freshly squeezed.

Colin [Smart] may not have looked too good, but I'm told he smelled lovely.
> STEVE SMITH, England captain, after the prop had allegedly collapsed after drinking aftershave at Paris banquet, 1982

It was about par for a rugby dinner . . . from what I can remember.
> COLIN SMART

> *The aftershave'll flow tonight.*
>
> STEVE SMITH after victory over Wales a month later

Who knows how many potential internationals were lost to the game forever when someone came up with the revolutionary idea that pre-match preparation should move from a haphazard assembly on Saturday lunchtime to tactical discussions in a rural hideaway hotel on a Friday night. Then it became Thursday night, then Thursday morning, then Wednesday evening . . . and now it all starts cranking up on Monday evening. A six-day build-up no less.

Rugby used to embrace, more than any other sport, the spirit of the comic book athlete, Alf Tupper – 'the Tough of the Track'. The usual script was for Alf to be up all night welding, then run about five miles to the stadium, pausing only to scoff a bagful of fish and chips on the way, before vaulting the spectator rail shortly after the starter's gun had gone off, and thrashing the field in his hobnail boots. The scenario now would be for Alf to be tucked up by 9 p.m., have a carefully prepared plate of pasta at the precise time ordered by his personal dietician, and be only momentarily distracted from the task in hand by negotiating a new adidas contract over the mobile.

The inclusion of Liam Botham, son of Ian, in England's 2000 summer touring squad, conjured up memories of the old man and his own form of legendary pre-match preparation. There was, and probably still is, a pub in Taunton (which had better remain nameless) whose unreasonably strict licensing hours involved calling last orders when the milkman arrived, by which time Botham senior – to use a cricketing analogy – had barely seen the shine off the new ball.

Ferocious batsman though he was, some of his more spectacular innings came against bowlers who had been unwise enough to accept his previous night's invitation to an evening out, and who were barely capable of completing their run up without retching, never mind thinking about how to get Botham out. Liam, though, is a product of a different generation, and perfectly suited to the demands of modern-day professional sport. As the old man put it, in his own fairly unsubtle style, when asked if Liam had inherited any of his own social staying power: 'You must be joking. He only has to smell a barmaid's fart and he's pissed.'

When Italy made their debut in last year's Home International Championship, the nationwide knowledge of rugby union was thin enough for their police force – previously weaned on visits from the England football team – to be trebled for the influx of boozed up England supporters. They were then left scratching their heads when not a single bar was trashed. It was a shame that Italy had not entered the fray twenty years earlier, when it would have been an education to watch the police busy monitoring the supporters, while the players were, in the time-honoured fashion of the day, running amok in various licensed premises – an eternal piss-up in the Eternal City.

The contact between player and supporter was also a crucial ingredient of rugby union in days gone by. When a chap wearing a kilt disappeared under some table in Edinburgh, he would have a decent chance of finding the space already occupied by a member of the side he had spent the afternoon cheering on, and at club level, part of the attraction for the supporter was to have his post-match pint pulled by the home scrum half. It didn't matter how many caps he might have won, no one was too big a name to go on the bar rota.

Go into a rugby union clubhouse today, however, and there won't be a player in sight. They usually make their way straight from dressing room to sponsors' lounge, where they acknowledge their gratitude to the money men by allowing themselves to be bored rigid by Algernon from accounts, and thence on to the private players' bar, where the only people involved in dangerous levels of consumption are the old players turned committee men.

The media likewise now have to go through a variety of official channels to make any kind of contact with a player, other than via the permanently turned off mobile phone or statutory agent. Training sessions are invariably closed, with a small selection of players made available for interview at times of the management's choosing. The legendary camaraderie between player and press man barely exists any more, and journalists who have caused offence now become excluded from interviews rather than suffer their traditional fate of being thrown fully clothed into the after-match bath. It was once part of a cub reporter's essential training to conduct his Saturday night press conference while immersed in several gallons of mud and scum.

One of the more bizarre items issued to modern international rugby players in recent years have been laptop computers, an idea promoted by the England coach Clive Woodward in order to maintain an interactive wavelength for swapping tactical ideas, diet sheets, and a variety of clerical instructions. This actually helped to rekindle the spirit of the old days because all it actually promoted was a literacy in playing computer games, and a familiarity with the Internet which resulted in players downloading a variety of dubious material to each other from their hotel rooms. The phone bill from England's 1999 tour to Australia was far larger than anything paid out in hotel damages in the old amateur days.

I will offer you a comparison between some of England's written schedules for the year 2000 and the year 1970. The latter is made up because they didn't exist in those days, but the fictitious version certainly has the ring of accuracy about it.

2000: Lloyds TSB Six Nations Championship:
England v Ireland
1970: Five Nations Championship (unsponsored):
England v Ireland

2000: Tuesday, 1 February

12.15–12.45 p.m. RFU Schools Pack and Six Nations Exhibition Launch, Museum of Rugby, Twickenham.

Team Announcement. Clive Woodward. 1.15–1.30 Spirit of Rugby Lounge, Twickenham.

1.45–2.30 p.m. One-One interviews with all players.

2.30 p.m. Open Training – warm-up session only Twickenham.

1970: Tuesday, 1 February

12.15–12.45 p.m. Bricklayers' Arms. RFU six pack, to be consumed by all players, and Five Nations launch of punt down the Thames, with all players behaving extremely schoolboyishly, and everyone getting wet.

Team Announcement. 1.15–1.30 p.m. Receive phone call at work from reporter from *Surrey Comet* asking if you're in the team for Saturday. Reply: 'Haven't heard anything, but will occasionally be leaving the lathe to listen to the radio sports bulletins.'

2.30 p.m. Open Training – warm-up session only. Try running to a pub further away for a late lunchtime pint (last orders 3 p.m.) instead of walking to the one next door.

2000: Wednesday

2.30 p.m. Open training – warm-up session only, Pennyhill Park Hotel, Bagshot, Surrey.

1970: Wednesday

2.30 p.m. Open training – warm-up session only. Nip home to the wife (or go round to the girlfriend's if more strenuous exercise required) for a few indoor press-ups.

2000: Thursday

10.30–11 a.m. Captain's press conference, team hotel.

11.00–11.30 a.m. One-one interviews with captain and three players, Pennyhill Park, Balmoral Room.

1970: Thursday
10.30–11 a.m. Captain's press conference. Answer phone to any reporter who might call you at work. Not that you'll have a clue what the team is.

11–11.30 p.m. One-one interviews with captain and three players by local CID who have reason to believe you may be able to assist with inquiries re broken tables and stolen dartboard at the Fox and Firkin

2000: Friday
11–11.45 a.m. Clive Woodward press conference. Pennyhill Park Hotel, Eaton Suite.

1970: Friday
11–11.45 a.m. Coach available for one-one telephone calls at Arkwright the Plumbers, Workers Canteen, assuming he's still around for his tea break, and not been called out on an emergency burst-pipe job.

2000: PLEASE NOTE
If you wish to attend the open training warm-up session on Tuesday, please contact Sarah Shelley in the Communications Department on 020 8831 6626 by 5 p.m. on Monday, 13 March. Times, dates and venues may be subject to change.

1970: PLEASE NOTE
Please contact Sean the barman at the clubhouse for any further information. Times, dates and venues may be subject to change, depending on whether people are away on holiday.

It would, of course, be foolish to suggest that rugby is not faster, more physical, and more skilful than it was years ago, but there is one scene I can still picture now from a top club game in the early 1980s that would never be witnessed today.

Two opposing, freshly scarred and battered prop forwards, surrounded by supporters from both sides, were standing at the bar discussing the events that had allowed them to enjoy, courtesy of the referee, first use of the bath.

'Bloody hell, I never saw that one coming. I'll have a look on the 25 yard line later for that missing tooth.'

'I'm sorry, you'll have to speak up. I think you burst my eardrum with that left hook.'

And with that, the first one turned to the other and said, 'Now then, you dirty bastard. What are you having?'